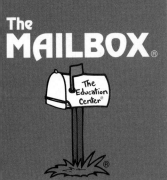

The MAILBOX®

The Education Center®

grades 2-3

Organize SEPTEMBER Now!™

Everything You Need for a Successful September

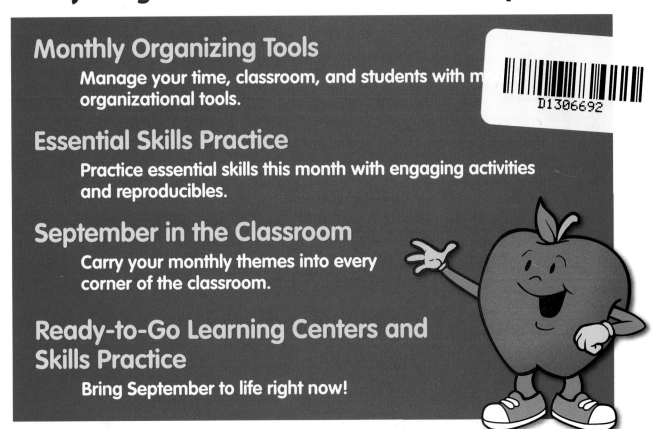

Monthly Organizing Tools

Manage your time, classroom, and students with m̶͟͟͟ organizational tools.

Essential Skills Practice

Practice essential skills this month with engaging activities and reproducibles.

September in the Classroom

Carry your monthly themes into every corner of the classroom.

Ready-to-Go Learning Centers and Skills Practice

Bring September to life right now!

Managing Editor: Debra Liverman

Editorial Team: Becky S. Andrews, Kimberley Bruck, Karen P. Shelton, Diane Badden, Thad H. McLaurin, Sharon Murphy, Cindy K. Daoust, Peggy Hambright, Sherry McGregor, Amy Payne, Hope Taylor Spencer, Karen A. Brudnak, Sarah Hamblet, Hope Rodgers, Dorothy C. McKinney, Cindy Barber, Amy Barsanti, Anita Batt, Tammie Bennett, Deborah P. Campbell, Virginia Conrad, Colleen Dabney, Stacie Stone Davis, Kelly Decoteau, Julie Douglas, Jean Erickson, Ann Fisher, Tammy Geiger, Kelli L. Gowdy, David Green, Terry Healy, Linda Holman, Vicki Lopez, Kim Minafo, Jenice Pearson, Anne Sharp

Production Team: Lisa K. Pitts, Pam Crane, Rebecca Saunders, Jennifer Tipton Cappoen, Chris Curry, Sarah Foreman, Theresa Lewis Goode, Clint Moore, Greg D. Rieves, Barry Slate, Donna K. Teal, Zane Williard, Tazmen Carlisle, Amy Kirtley-Hill, Cathy Edwards Simrell, Lynette Dickerson, Mary Rainey, Angela Kamstra

www.themailbox.com

©2006 The Mailbox®
All rights reserved.
ISBN #1-56234-667-9

Manufactured in the United States
10 9 8 7 6 5 4 3 2 1

Table of Contents

Monthly Organizing Tools

A collection of reproducible forms, notes, and other just-for-September timesavers and organizational tools.

Essential Skills Practice

Fun, skill-building activities and reproducibles that combine the skills your students must learn with favorite September themes.

September in the Classroom

In a hurry to find a specific type of September activity? It's right here!

Ready-to-Go Learning Centers and Skills Practice

Two preprinted center activities you can tear out and use almost instantly! Plus a collection of additional reproducible skill builders and 8 preprinted student activity cards!

Answer Keys

Skills Grid

	Back-to-School	Open House	Apples	Grandparents	Centers	Games	Time Fillers	Writing Ideas & Prompts	Learning Center The Good Apple	Learning Center Bubba's Buse	Ready-to-Go Practice	Activity Cards
Language Arts												
initial consonant blends					56							
vowel sounds							66					
long and short *a*			36									
compound words												91
rhyming words												91
vocabulary							67					91
parts of speech	19											
identifying nouns and verbs											86	
plural nouns			38			61					85	
sequencing			42									
recalling details			39									
summarizing					57							
listening						60						
listening, speaking	21											
writing sentences	18							69				
writing descriptive sentences			37									
capitalization	20, 28			47							87	
ending punctuation								69			89	
beginning capitals and end marks										78		
writing a friendly letter		30		44								
journal prompts								68				
creative writing				44				68				
planning a story												91
Math												
number awareness							66					93
number sense							66					
place value			37			61					88	
comparing numbers					57							93
ordering whole numbers											84	
addition facts to 18	27											
basic facts					56	60						93
fact families				45					72			
column addition			43									
addition and subtraction			36									
two-digit addition without regrouping				46								
two-digit addition with regrouping	29											
two-digit addition with and without regrouping	18											
two-digit subtraction without regrouping											90	
counting money	21											
graphing	20		38									
bar graphs		31										
telling time	19											
nonstandard measurement												93
Science												
making predictions			39									
Other												
self-esteem		31										

TEC60984

Notice

©The Mailbox® • *September Monthly Organizers* • TEC60984

Clip art: Use the artwork on student papers and on correspondence such as announcements, forms, and parent notes.

September

Sunday	Monday	Tuesday	Wednesday	Thursday	Friday	Saturday

CENTER CHECKLIST

Writing Center

Name

Class List

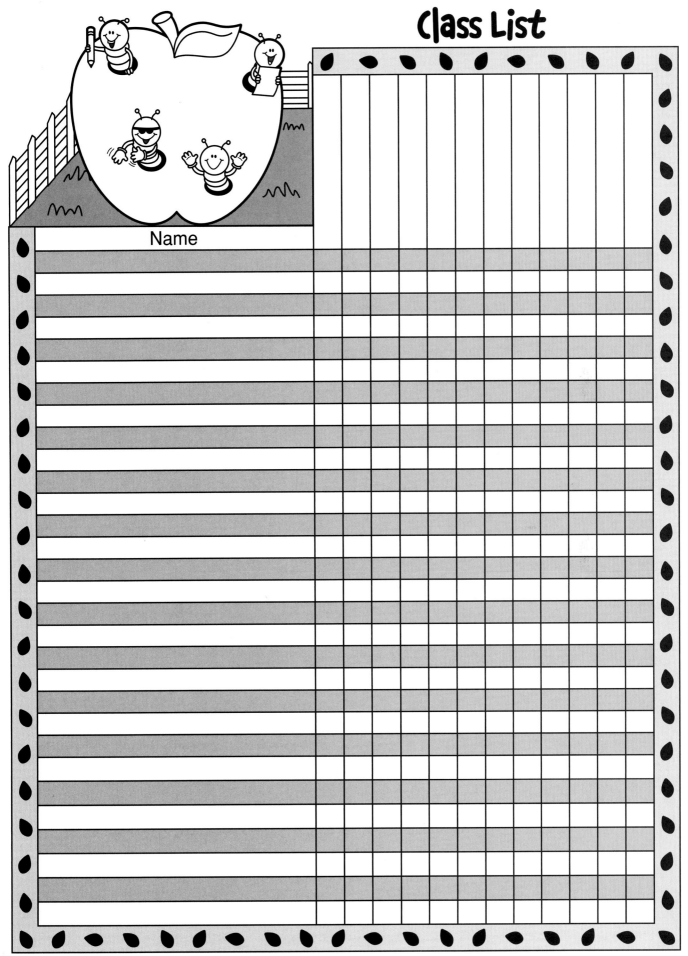

Name

Classroom News

From _____

Date _____

Check Out What We're Learning

Superstars

Special Thanks

Please Remember

Help Wanted

Classroom News

From _____

Date _____

We are rooting for you!

Name_____

Goal _____

_____

©The Mailbox® • *September Monthly Organizers* • TEC60984

Name_____

Goal _____

_____

You can do it!

©The Mailbox® • *September Monthly Organizers* • TEC60984

Incentive charts: Have students track their progress as they work toward a variety of goals.

_____'s

Journal

Word Bank

apple	delicious	grow	red
bake	eat	juicy	school
climb	fall	pick	sweet
crunchy	green	pie	yellow

©The Mailbox® • *September Monthly Organizers* • TEC60984

Journal cover: Make this page the front cover of your students' writing journals. Encourage authors to refer to the handy word bank for instant inspiration.

Birthdays & Special Days:

To Do:

- ★ _____
- ★ _____
- ★ _____
- ★ _____
- ★ _____
- ★ _____
- ★ _____
- ★ _____
- ★ _____
- ★ _____
- ★ _____
- ★ _____
- ★ _____
- ★ _____

Meetings:

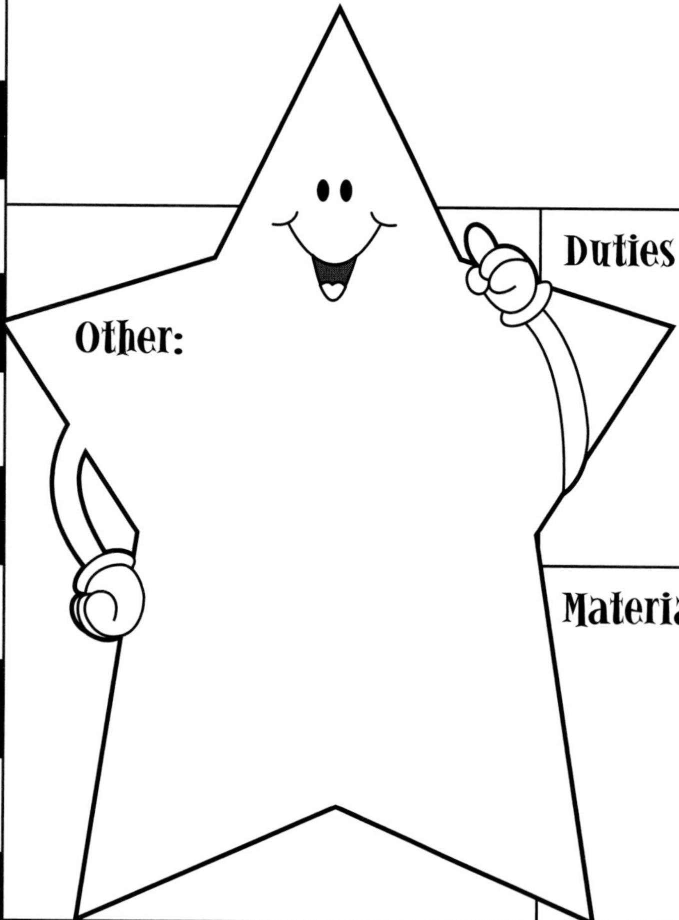

Other:

Duties This Month:

Materials to Collect:

Monthly planning form: Use this handy form to stay on top of each month's school-related responsibilities.

Open: Use this page for parent correspondence, and use it with students too. For example, design a word search on the page that contains each of your students' names and make copies of it for the class to complete.

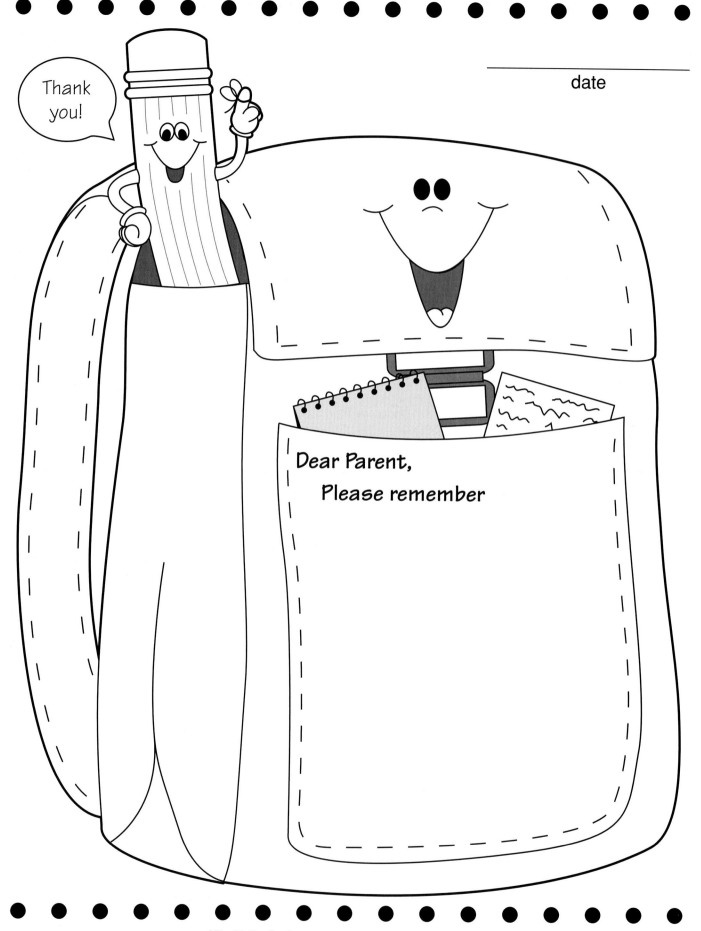

date

Thank you!

Dear Parent,

Please remember

Parent reminder note: Use this note to remind parents of supply requests, field trips, and special events such as classroom presentations, school programs, or guest speakers.

School Note

School Note

School notes: Use these notes for parent correspondence such as announcing an upcoming event, requesting supplies or volunteers, and writing messages of praise.

Please help your child decorate this apple for our "good apple" display. First, spend time together cutting words from newspapers and magazines that describe your child's likes, interests, and personality. Then have your child cut out the apple and glue the words on it. Last, help your child design a unique apple leaf and glue it to the stem. Be creative!

We hope to see your completed project by _____.

Sincerely,

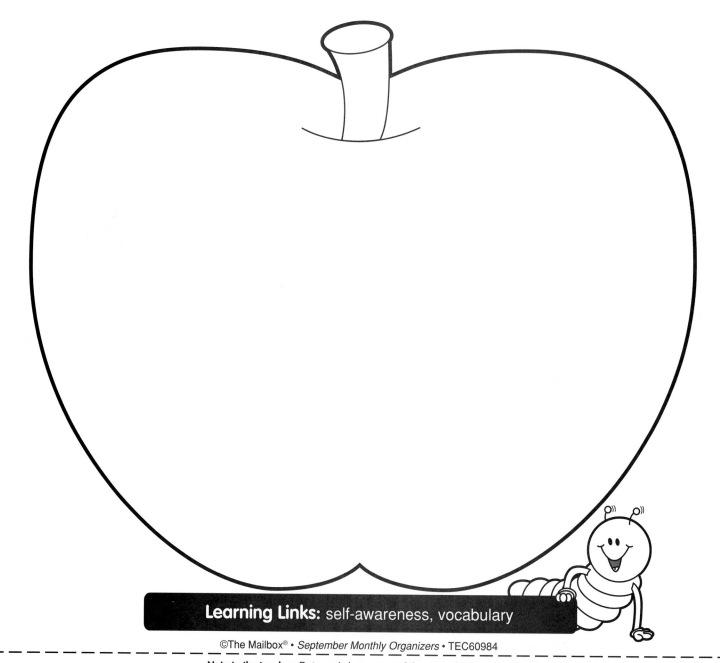

Learning Links: self-awareness, vocabulary

©The Mailbox® • *September Monthly Organizers* • TEC60984

Note to the teacher: Date and sign a copy of the page. Make student copies on colorful construction paper; then use a marker to write each child's name on an apple. When a child returns her project, help her share it with the class. Then post it on a display titled "A Bushel of Good Apples!"

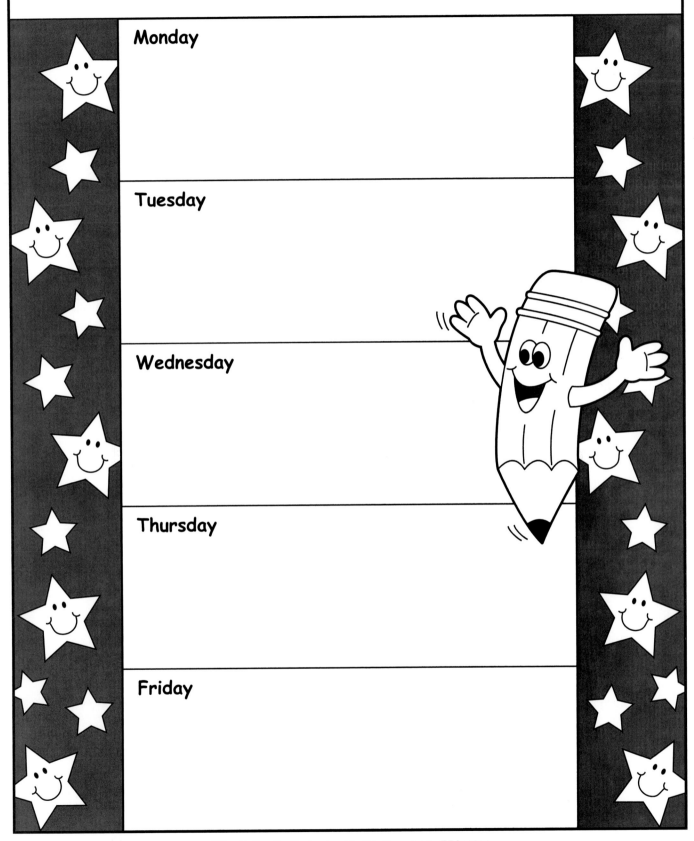

HOMEWORK FOR THE WEEK

OF _____

Monday

Tuesday

Wednesday

Thursday

Friday

Homework organizer: Program a copy of this form with homework assignments for the week or have each child write his assignments on a blank form.

Back-to-School

Language Arts

Writing sentences

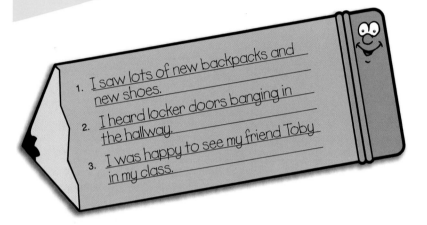

1. I saw lots of new backpacks and new shoes.
2. I heard locker doors banging in the hallway.
3. I was happy to see my friend Toby in my class.

First-Day Experiences

Assess students' writing skills with this quick idea. On the second or third day of school, lead a class discussion about the sights and sounds that students observed on the first day of school. Then have each student write three sentences about her first-day experiences on a copy of the pencil pattern on page 22. Have her color and cut out her pencil; then provide time for each child to share her favorite sentence with the class. Post the completed pencils on a display titled "We Are Sharp Writers!"

Two-digit addition with and without regrouping

Math

The Numbers on the Bus

To prepare this partner center, color and cut out a copy of the bus pattern on page 22. Also cut each of three small index cards into fourths. Program each of the 12 resulting smaller cards with a different two-digit number. Place all the cutouts in a resealable plastic bag at a center along with writing paper. A pair visiting the center randomly selects two cards and places them on the bus pattern. Then each student adds the numbers on his paper and compares his answer to his partner's. Together they resolve any conflicting answers. The pair continues solving problems until all the cards have been used.

Welcome your eager youngsters back to school with these fresh activities and reproducibles!

Parts of speech

Get-to-Know-You Puzzles

Guide each student through the directions below to make a personalized puzzle using a copy of the grid on page 23. Then collect and redistribute the puzzles, being sure that no child receives her own. Each student solves the puzzle and then tries to guess the identity of its creator. After matching each puzzle to its owner, have each child mount her puzzle on construction paper and write her name at the top. Post the puzzles on a bulletin board titled "Puzzled No More!"

Directions:
1. On lines 1–3, write three adjectives that describe you.
2. On lines 4–6, write three nouns that name places that you like.
3. On lines 7–9, write three verbs that tell things that you like to do.
4. On lines 10–12, write three nouns that name people who are special to you.
5. Use all capital letters to write the words across or up and down anywhere in the grid.
6. Fill in the empty boxes with capital letters.

Kinsey

? ? Mystery Student ? ?

1. friendly
2. funny
3. helpful
4. beach
5. home
6. school
7. run
8. swim
9. learn
10. Granny
11. Grandpa
12. John

Math

Telling time

Our Class Schedule

Write your daily schedule on chart paper. Next to each subject, write its beginning and ending times. Have each student write his name, the subjects, and the times on a copy of page 24. Then invite student volunteers to model the beginning and ending times on a large display clock. For each subject, have each student draw clock hands on her paper to match the corresponding beginning and ending times. Encourage students to keep their schedules handy so they'll know exactly what's coming up!

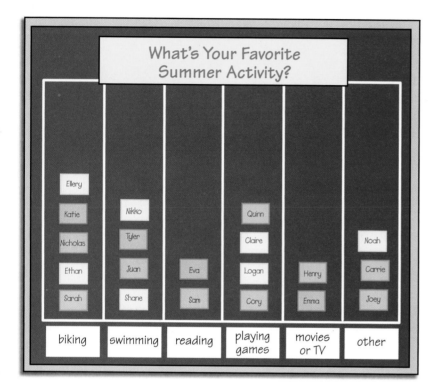

What's Your Favorite?

Students learn more about their class-mates with this daily graphing activity. Draw the chart shown on a bulletin board. Then, as a class, brainstorm a list of questions that students would like to have answered about each other, such as "What is your favorite hobby?" and "What is your favorite food?" List the questions on a sheet of paper and store them near the graph along with some sticky notes. Each morning, program a lami-nated sentence strip with one question and laminated index cards with several answer choices. Post the strip and cards on the graph as shown. Then invite each child to write his name on a sticky note and place the note in the appropriate column. Later in the day, spend a few minutes discussing the graph's data.

Capitalizing proper nouns • • • • • • • • • • • • • • • • •

Language Arts

Birthdays on Display

This nifty activity gives each child the opportunity to announce her birthday! Give each child a copy of the birthday cake pattern on page 25 and access to a calendar for the current school year. Each child completes the sentences on the pattern, using capital letters where neces-sary. Then she decorates and cuts out the cake. Display the cakes as a year-round reminder of each child's special day!

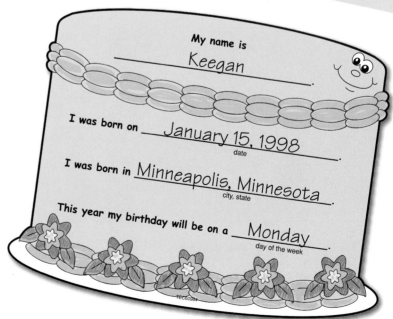

Buddy Ball

Invite students to sit in a circle on the floor for this listening game. Tell students to listen carefully as you have each child say his name and tell one interesting fact about himself. Next, hold a large beach ball as you reintroduce one student to the class by telling his name and repeating the fact that he revealed. Then toss the ball to that child; it's his turn to introduce another classmate and toss her the ball. Continue play until each child has had a turn.

Marie likes to ride her scooter.

Math • • • • • • • • • • • • • • Counting money

Let's Go School Shopping!

Prepare a three-player game by cutting apart the game cards from a construction paper copy of page 26. Make the cards self-checking by programming the back of each card with the amount of money shown on the card's front. Place the cards in a resealable bag and then guide players through the directions below.

Directions:
1. Stack the cards money or text side up. Player 1 draws a card. If it is a money card, he tells the amount shown and turns it over to check his answer. If correct, he keeps the card. If not, he returns the card to the bottom of the deck. If Player 1 draws a text card instead, he follows the directions on the card and then sets the card aside.
2. Player 2 and Player 3 each take a turn.
3. Continue play until all of the cards have been drawn. The player with the most cards at the end is the winner.

Find reproducible activities on pages 27–29.

Pencil Pattern
Use with "First-Day Experiences" on page 18.

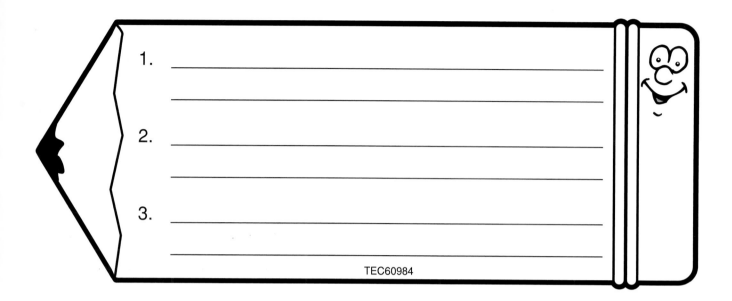

1. _____
2. _____
3. _____

TEC60984

Bus Pattern
Use with "The Numbers on the Bus" on page 18.

TEC60984

Mystery Student

1. _____
2. _____
3. _____
4. _____
5. _____
6. _____
7. _____
8. _____
9. _____
10. _____
11. _____
12. _____

©The Mailbox® • *September Monthly Organizers* • TEC60984

 _____'s

Daily Schedule

Subject	Begins	Ends
_____	_____:_____	_____:_____
_____	_____:_____	_____:_____
_____	_____:_____	_____:_____
_____	_____:_____	_____:_____
_____	_____:_____	_____:_____
_____	_____:_____	_____:_____
_____	_____:_____	_____:_____

Note to the teacher: Use with "Our Class Schedule" on page 19.

My name is

I was born on

date

I was born in

city, state

This year my birthday will be on a

day of the week

TEC60984

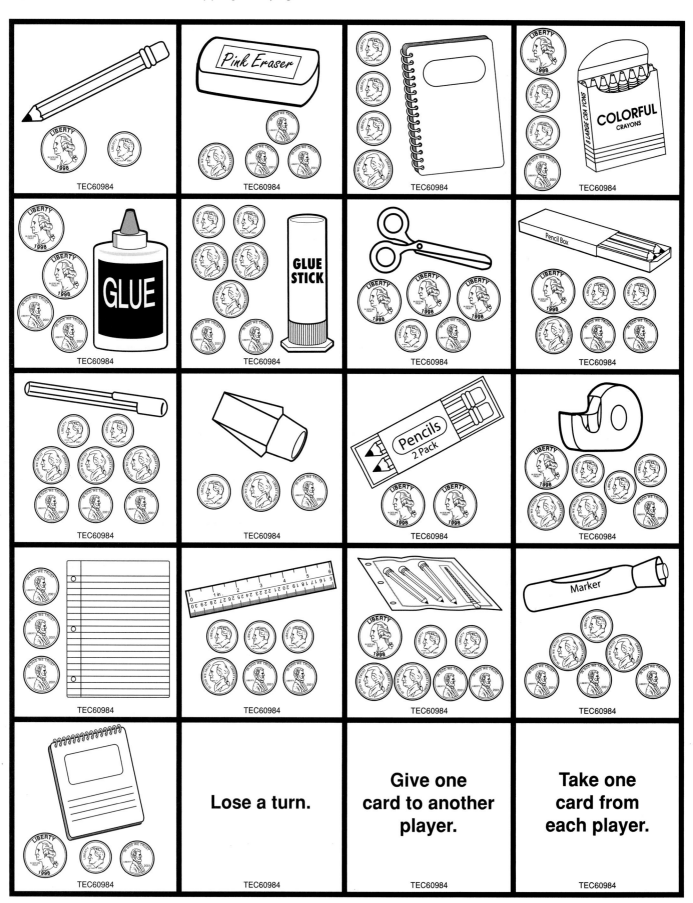

Where's My Bus?

Name _____   Date _____

Help the cubs find their bus.
Solve the first math fact in each row.
Color the fact in the row that has the
   same answer.
The first one has been done for you.

9 + 7 = _16_	6 + 7	8 + 8	8 + 4	9 + 4
6 + 6 = ____	8 + 5	6 + 8	5 + 7	1 + 5
5 + 6 = ____	3 + 6	7 + 4	9 + 4	6 + 7
6 + 8 = ____	9 + 5	3 + 6	4 + 9	5 + 5
5 + 7 = ____	6 + 6	9 + 0	8 + 3	9 + 2
3 + 4 = ____	4 + 4	2 + 5	7 + 8	6 + 6
4 + 6 = ____	5 + 3	7 + 3	3 + 8	7 + 1
7 + 7 = ____	4 + 9	2 + 5	8 + 6	2 + 8
8 + 3 = ____	7 + 6	8 + 8	5 + 9	6 + 5
1 + 5 = ____	2 + 8	4 + 7	3 + 3	9 + 2
9 + 8 = ____	5 + 5	8 + 9	7 + 3	6 + 0
3 + 6 = ____	2 + 7	7 + 7	5 + 2	4 + 4

Name _____

Date _____

We're Back and We're Busy!

Circle each letter that should be capitalized.
Color a matching eraser.

1. There is no school on labor day.

2. Ms. stone's class visited the pumpkin patch on tuesday.

3. Every wednesday, mr. Jones visits our classroom.

4. bring a book to share each day in october!

5. open house will be at 7:00 on monday.

6. Mr. lee's class will visit the firehouse on october 7.

7. The school will serve pizza each friday in september.

8. bring snacks for your class on september 24.

9. We will have a fall party on the last friday in october.

10. help us clean the playground on saturday.

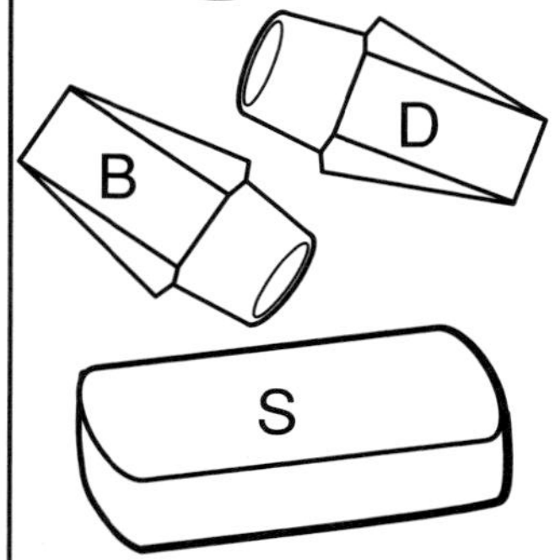

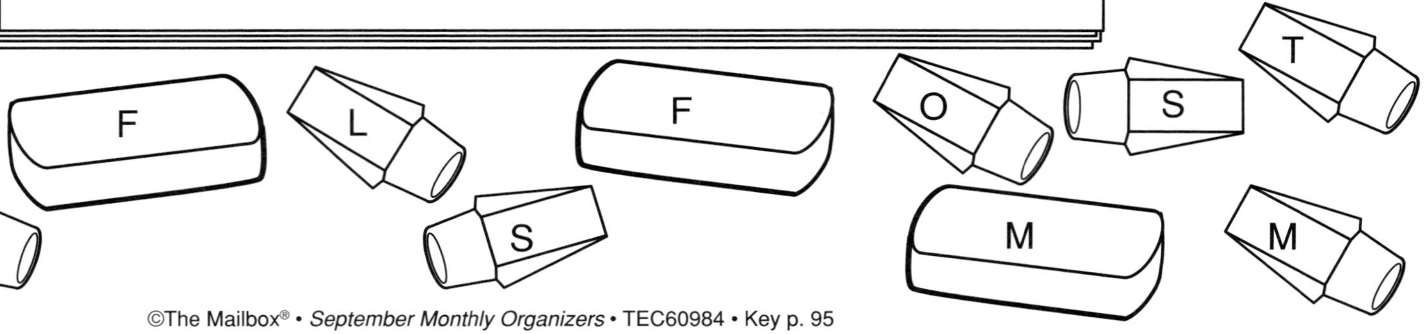

L   B   O   D   B   S   T   M   S   S   M   O   F   S   L   F   O   H   W   S

Capitalization

Walking to School

Name _____ Date _____

Add.
Help Max and Meg get to school.
If the answer is greater than 60, color the stone.

| 28 | 65 | 34 | 27 | 19 |
| + 36 | + 17 | + 28 | + 43 | + 32 |

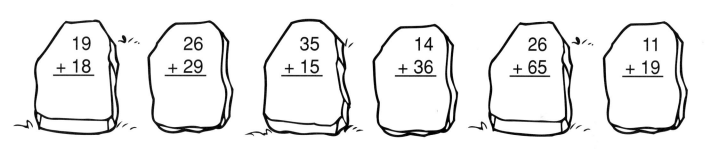

| 19 | 26 | 35 | 14 | 26 | 11 |
| + 18 | + 29 | + 15 | + 36 | + 65 | + 19 |

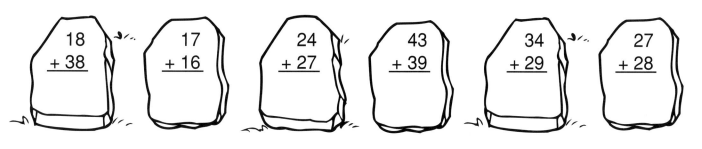

| 18 | 17 | 24 | 43 | 34 | 27 |
| + 38 | + 16 | + 27 | + 39 | + 29 | + 28 |

| 37 | 25 | 19 | 29 |
| + 19 | + 25 | + 35 | + 52 |

Two-Digit Addition With Regrouping 29

Open House

Management • • • • • • • • • • • • Parent communication

Magnet Pals

Exchange important contact information with these handy pens! Program a copy of the teacher pen pattern on page 33 so parents will know how to reach you at school. Copy a class supply of the programmed pattern on light-colored paper and laminate them. Cut out the pens and attach a magnetic strip to the back of each one. During open house, distribute the pens along with parent pens made from the pattern on page 33. Ask parents to fill out their pens and return them to you to file. Then suggest that they use the laminated teacher pens as fridge magnets.

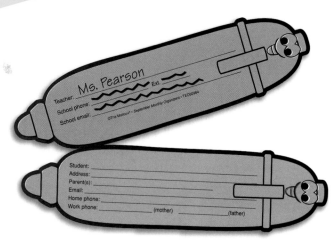

Teacher: Ms. Pearson   Ext.
School phone:
School email:
©The Mailbox® • September Monthly Organizer • TEC60984

Student:
Address:
Parent(s):
Email:
Home phone:
Work phone: _____ (mother) _____ (father)

Friendly letters • • • • • • • • • • • • • • **Language Arts**

Getting the Scoop!

Give parents a chance to get to know you by reading letters written by their children! Before open house, have students interview you to learn about your hobbies, family, other interests, and school duties. Invite each child to write his parent a letter to share what he learned. If desired, also have him draw and cut out a picture of you. Have him tape his letter to the picture and leave it on his desktop for open house. That night, invite each parent to sit at his child's desk and read the personalized introduction.

September 7

Dear Mom and Dad,
   My teacher is Ms. Smith. She can knit. She can also play the piano. Her two sons like soccer. Ms. Smith taught third grade for ten years. She has taught second grade for three years. She likes to teach reading and science best. I think it will be a fun year.

   Your son,
   Matt

Generate a buzz about your classroom hive and the new school year with this sweet collection of ideas!

Handy Attributes

This parent-child activity results in an attractive classroom display. In advance, place scissors, markers, and a sheet of light-colored construction paper at each child's desk. During open house, each parent traces her child's hand on the paper and then labels each finger of the tracing with one of her child's qualities. Next, each child traces her parent's hand on the paper and labels each finger of the tracing with one of her parent's qualities. Finally, the parent and child cut out the tracings and post them as a pair on a display titled "Together We Can 'Hand-le' Anything!"

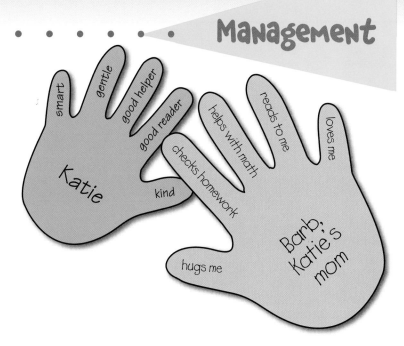

Parent Poll

Collect data from parents for a quick graphing lesson! Place a supply of question strips from page 34 along with a collection container on a table before open house. That night, invite each parent to fill out a strip and drop it in the container. The next day, tally the votes as a class. Then have each student use a copy of the graph pattern on page 34 to create a bar graph displaying the results. Afterward, discuss the graphs with questions such as the following: Which sweet treat do most parents prefer? Which do they least prefer? How could this data help someone buy refreshments for next year's open house?

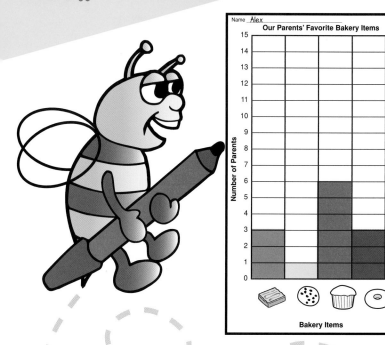

Carryout Bags

Send home open house materials (and a few surprises) in these student-designed bags. Have each child use permanent markers and stickers to decorate and personalize a gallon-sized resealable bag to leave on his desk before going home the afternoon of open house. That night, place a sticker, pencil, lollipop, and other assorted treats in each bag. Invite each parent to sit at his or her child's desk and then use the bag to carry home any materials and forms that you distribute. Children will be tickled by the unexpected surprises, and they can use the bags to return any needed forms to you the next morning!

Desktop Notes

A personal note from Mom and Dad is the perfect surprise the morning after open house! Before open house, place a sheet of decorative notepaper on each student's desk. That night, explain to parents that the notepaper is for them to write a special note to their child. Encourage parents to give positive feedback about the student's work and her classroom. After open house, write a quick note for those students whose parents could not attend. Students will be greeted by the inspirational notes the next morning!

Ashley,
We really enjoyed meeting your teacher and seeing your classroom. What a beautiful project you created! We're so proud. Have a great day!

Mom and Dad

Use with “Magnet Pals” on page 30.

teacher pen

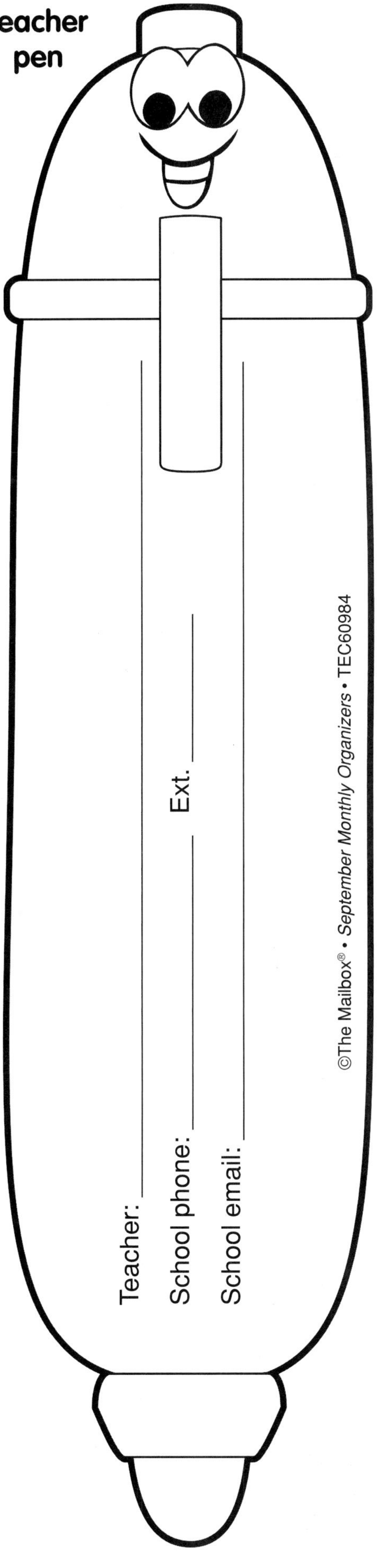
Teacher: ______
School phone: ______ Ext. ______
School email: ______
©The Mailbox® • *September Monthly Organizers* • TEC60984

parent pen

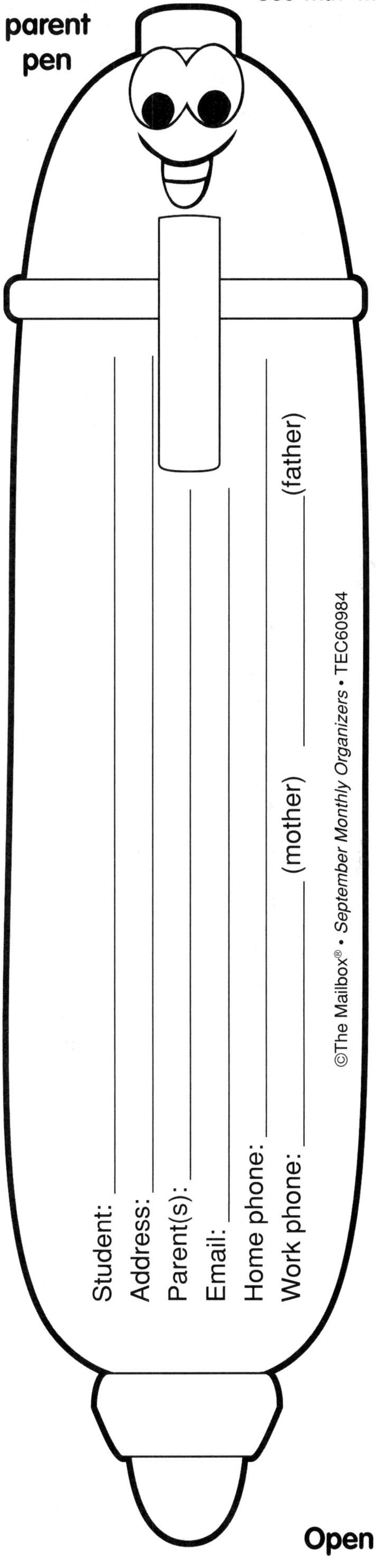
Student: ______
Address: ______
Parent(s): ______
Email: ______
Home phone: ______
Work phone: ______ (mother) ______ (father)
©The Mailbox® • *September Monthly Organizers* • TEC60984

Which of the following is your favorite sweet treat: brownie, cookie, cupcake, or doughnut? _____

TEC60984

Which of the following is your favorite sweet treat: brownie, cookie, cupcake, or doughnut? _____

TEC60984

Which of the following is your favorite sweet treat: brownie, cookie, cupcake, or doughnut? _____

TEC60984

Bar Graph Pattern
Use with "Parent Poll" on page 31.

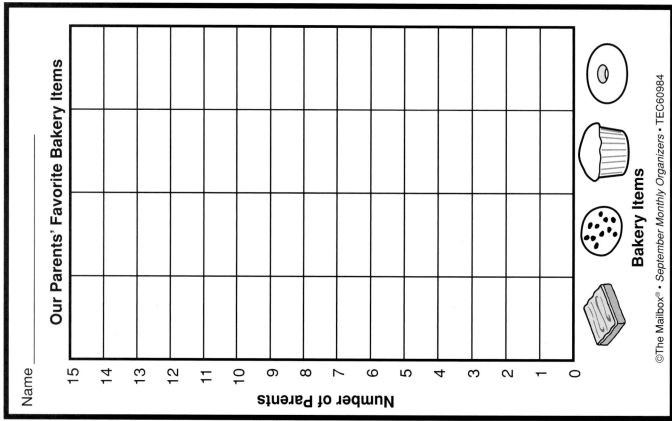

©The Mailbox® • *September Monthly Organizers* • TEC60984

Have you heard the buzz?

We're having an open house

on _____,
　　　　　　　　　　　　　 day

_____ at _____.
　　　date　　　　　　　　　　　time

We hope to see you there!

_____
　　　　　　teacher

©The Mailbox® • *September Monthly Organizers* • TEC60984

Have you heard the buzz?

We're having an open house

on _____,
　　　　　　　　　　　　　 day

_____ at _____.
　　　date　　　　　　　　　　　time

We hope to see you there!

_____
　　　　　　teacher

©The Mailbox® • *September Monthly Organizers* • TEC60984

Apples

Long and short a

Worms With Words

To prepare for this small-group activity, make two apple cards and a desired number of worm cards using the patterns on pages 40 and 41. Attach a picture or a sticker to each apple—one for short *a* and one for long *a*. Then program each worm card with a short *a* word or long *a* word and cut it out.

To begin, display the apple cutouts and stack the worm cards facedown. Students take turns drawing a card from the stack, reading aloud its word, and placing the card below the corresponding apple. When all the cards are sorted, lead students in reading each set of words.

Addition and subtraction

Math

Hand-Picked Problems

Computation and comparing numbers go hand in hand at this center! Make copies of page 41 on red and green construction paper. (Laminate the cards and cut them out.) Then program each apple with a one- or two-digit number. Store the apples in a basket along with lined paper. A student randomly removes two apples from the basket. If the cards are the same color, he adds the numbers on his paper. If the cards are different colors, he subtracts the smaller number from the larger number. He continues in this manner until he has two or three different problems. To vary the difficulty of the center, simply reprogram the apples.

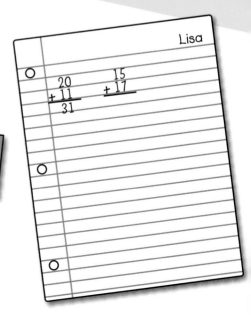

Pick from this collection of ideas that are ripe for bushels of learning!

Place value

Places, Please!

This whole-class game moves students' number skills in the right direction! Program a class set of construction paper apple cards (patterns on page 41) for place-value practice. Underline one digit in each numeral and then cut out the cards. Also label one sheet of paper for every place value being reviewed (ones, tens, etc.). Post each sign in a different area of the classroom.

To play, pass out the cards and say, "Apples, find your places." Each student identifies the place value of the underlined digit and moves to the corresponding classroom location. When students are in their places, ask every child to read his number to a classmate and verify the place value of his underlined numeral. For another round, collect and redistribute the cards.

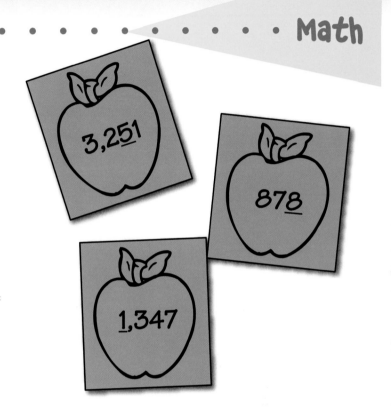

Language Arts

Writing descriptive sentences

Which Apple Is It?

Collect a variety of fresh apples that have distinguishing characteristics. Label each apple and display the apples where students can study them. Next, give each student a large index card. Have him secretly choose one of the apples and write three sentences to describe it. Invite each student to read his sentences and challenge the class to identify the apple being described. Afterward, have each student swap cards with a partner to check his sentences for correct capitalization and punctuation.

My apple has a short stem. My apple is greenish brown. There is a little dark spot near the bottom.

Language Arts

Sort 'em Out!

To set up this center, use a permanent marker to label two pie tins with the plural rules shown. Also make construction paper copies of the apple cards on page 41 and cut them out. Label each card with a singular noun. Prepare an answer key with the corresponding plurals listed by rule. Place the apples, the pie tins, the answer key, and lined paper at a center. A student sorts the apples by rule into the pie tins. Then, for each group of words, she writes the corresponding plurals on her paper. She uses the key to check her work.

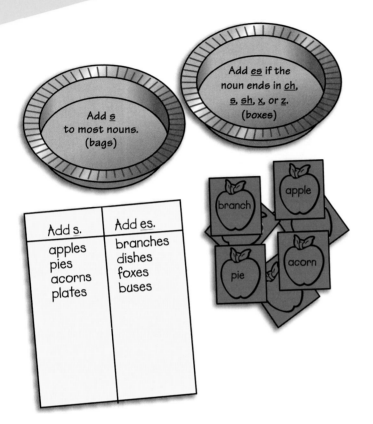

Add <u>s</u> to most nouns. (bags)

Add <u>es</u> if the noun ends in <u>ch</u>, <u>s</u>, <u>sh</u>, <u>x</u>, or <u>z</u>. (boxes)

Add s.	Add es.
apples	branches
pies	dishes
acorns	foxes
plates	buses

branch · apple · pie · acorn

Graphing

Math

Data Chomping

Get to the core of picture graphs with this activity. In advance, make a supply of apple core cards from the pattern page 40. Then brainstorm with students different foods that contain apples. Record their responses on chart paper. For one week, invite each student to write her name on an apple core card each time she eats one of the listed foods. On the back of the card, have her write the food she ate. Afterward, use the collected data to create a large picture graph. Extend the learning by generating questions for students to answer using the data on the graph.

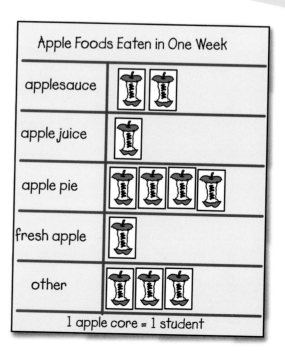

Apple Foods Eaten in One Week

applesauce	🍎🍎
apple juice	🍎
apple pie	🍎🍎🍎🍎
fresh apple	🍎
other	🍎🍎🍎

1 apple core = 1 student

What Do You Believe?

Share Steven Kellogg's *Johnny Appleseed* to show students what it means to really stretch the truth! Prepare a class supply of both red and green apples (patterns on page 41). Then read the story. Explain that tall tales like this one use exaggeration to make the story more interesting. As you reread the story, ask students to listen for examples of exaggeration and for what might be factual information. After reading, have each student write one fact from the story on a red apple and one exaggeration on a green apple. Display the apples on a tree-covered bulletin board titled "Really, Johnny?"

John Chapman was born in Massachusetts.

He almost got eaten by a giant fish.

Name Adam

My prediction:
I think the apple in water will not turn brown. The water will keep it white.

The apple in lemon juice did not turn brown. The lemon juice kept it white.

Find reproducible activities on pages 42–43.

Apple Observation

How do you keep apples from turning brown after being cut? Find out with this whole-class experiment. Label each of three bowls with one of the following: "water," "lemon juice," and "nothing." Fill one with water, fill another with lemon juice, and leave the third empty. Place a freshly cut apple slice in each bowl. State the contents of each bowl and give each child a copy of the apple slice pattern on page 40. Have him write a prediction on the pattern about which slice he thinks will take the longest to turn brown. Have students share their predictions. Check the apples every 30 minutes for two hours. Discuss any changes. *(After two hours, the slice covered in lemon juice should be the only one unchanged.)* Tell students that a sliced apple will turn brown. However, the acid in the lemon juice helps delay the browning process. If desired, continue the experiment to see how long it will take for the slice in the lemon juice to also turn brown. Finally, have students check their predictions by recording what actually happened on the back of their apple slices.

Apple Slice Pattern

Use with "Apple Observation" on page 39.

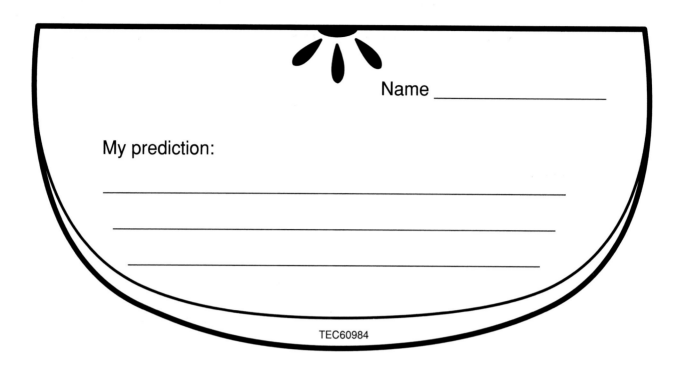

Name _____

My prediction:

_____

_____

_____

TEC60984

Apple Core Card

Use with "Data Chomping" on page 38.

TEC60984

Worm Patterns

Use with "Worms With Words" on page 36.

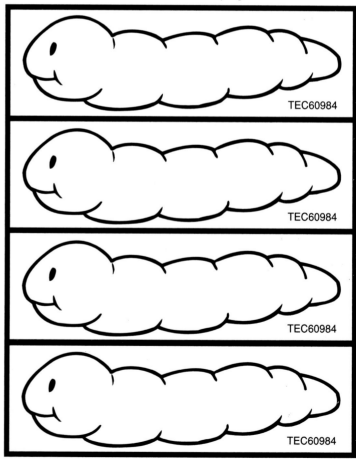

TEC60984

TEC60984

TEC60984

TEC60984

Use with "Worms With Words" and "Hand-Picked Problems" on page 36, "Places, Please!" on page 37, "Sort 'em Out!" on page 38, "What Do You Believe?" on page 39, "In the Bag" on page 56, "Fill the Tree!" on page 64, and "Number Builders" on page 66.

TEC60984 TEC60984
TEC60984 TEC60984
TEC60984 TEC60984

Applesauce Mix-Up

Name_____ Date _____

Cut out the strips.
Place the strips in order.
Glue the strips to the apple.

©The Mailbox® • *September Monthly Organizers* • TEC60984 • Key p. 95

Next, place the apple slices in a pot of water.

Then cut the apples into slices.

Mash the soft apples.

Finally, eat the applesauce.

First, peel the apples.

Boil the slices until they are soft.

Johnny's Surprise

Name _____

Date _____

?

Add.

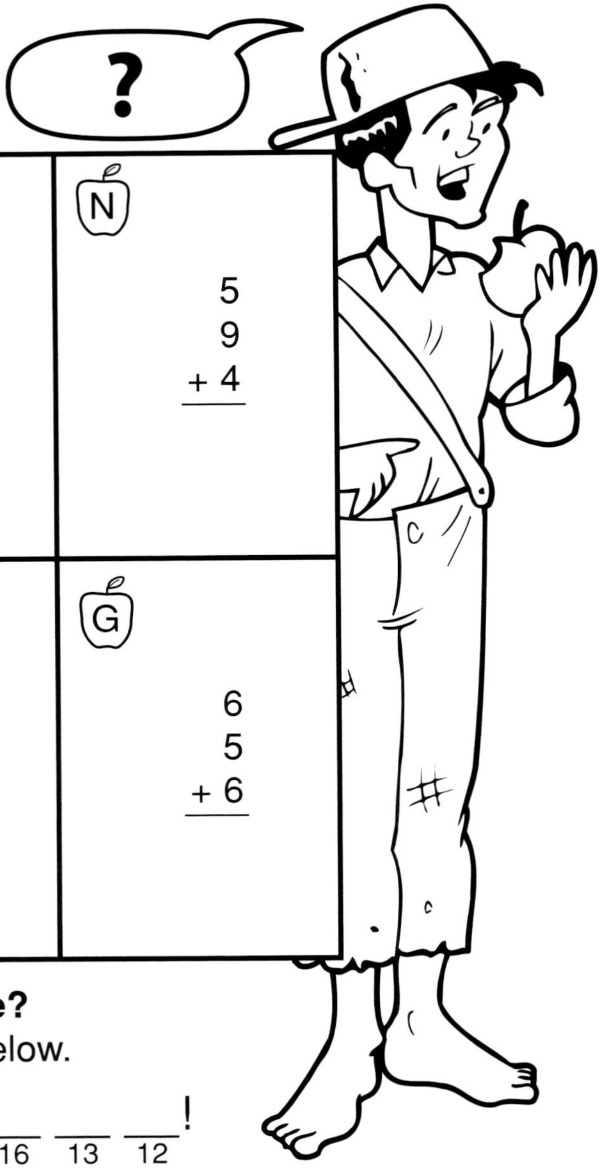

A 6 2 +3	**O** 9 0 +7	**L** 5 5 +5	**M** 1 3 +8	**I** 2 8 +0	**N** 5 9 +4
H 6 2 +1	**R** 7 4 +2	**F** 6 8 +5	**W** 3 1 +2	**D** 4 6 +4	**G** 6 5 +6

What is worse than finding a worm in your apple?

To solve the riddle, match the letters to the answers below.

19 10 18 14   10 18 17   9 11 15 19   9 11   6 16 13 12 !

Grandparents

Celebrate grandparents and other senior adults on National Grandparents Day (annually the first Sunday after Labor Day) with these grand ideas and reproducibles!

Language Arts

Writing a friendly letter

Mailable Hugs

After reviewing the format of a friendly letter, give each student a sheet of writing paper. Each child writes a letter to a grandparent or senior friend and signs it "With a big hug, [child's name]." Next, he accordion-folds two 12" x 18" construction paper strips and glues one strip to each side of his paper. Then the student traces his hands on the same color paper, cuts out the tracings, and glues them to the ends of the strips as shown. Help him fold the letter (enclosing the hands and arms inside) and place it in a large envelope. Send the letters home with a note encouraging parents to mail the hugs to their addressees.

September 9

Dear Grandma,
Today we read a book about grandparents. I had a taco for lunch. Then we played Red Light, Green Light at recess. I miss you.

With a big hug,

Jonathan

Creative writing

Language Arts

Grand Recipes

Get cooking with recipes that tell what makes grandparents so special. Have children brainstorm words that describe their grandmothers, grandfathers, or senior friends. Next, discuss the parts of a recipe and some basic measurements such as a cup, a teaspoon, and a pinch. Then give each child a large index card. Guide her to write a recipe that includes ingredients and directions to make her special grandparent. Once it's complete, have her decorate a large cookie cutout to resemble her grandparent or senior friend. Display the cookies and recipes on a bulletin board titled "Grand Recipes."

Recipe for Grandma Bea

Ingredients:
1 c. laughter
2 tsp. singing
1 lb. kindness
3 c. love
pinch of funny jokes

Put the laughter and singing in a bowl. Stir. Add the kindness. Let it sit for five minutes. Add the love. Sprinkle the funny jokes on top. Mix it all up. Do not spill any! Then shape into the best grandma ever.

Find reproducible activities on pages 45–47.

Grandpa's Hats

Name _____ Date _____

Add and subtract.

10 − 2 = ___   13 − 9 = ___   11 − 5 = ___

8 + 2 = ___   4 + 9 = ___   6 + 5 = ___

10 − 8 = ___   13 − 4 = ___   11 − 6 = ___

2 + 8 = ___   9 + 4 = ___   5 + 6 = ___

17 − 8 = ___   12 − 3 = ___   14 − 6 = ___

9 + 8 = ___   9 + 3 = ___   8 + 6 = ___

17 − 9 = ___   12 − 9 = ___   14 − 8 = ___

8 + 9 = ___   3 + 9 = ___   6 + 8 = ___

13 − 7 = ___   15 − 9 = ___

6 + 7 = ___   6 + 9 = ___

13 − 6 = ___   15 − 6 = ___

7 + 6 = ___   9 + 6 = ___

Grandma Betty's 100th Birthday!

Name _____   Date _____

Add.
Color the matching answer.

1.   34
      + 21

2.   21
      + 17

3.   37
      + 52

4.   52
      + 34

5.   65
      + 22

6.   33
      + 16

7.   30
      + 18

8.   59
      + 20

9.   43
      + 16

10.   46
      + 32

11.   42
      + 15

12.   30
      + 36

A Grand Trip

Name _____   Date _____

Write each city and state using correct capitalization.

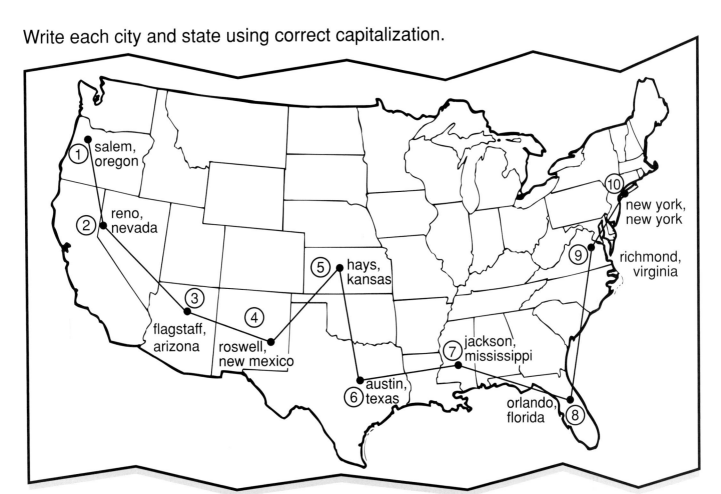

1. _____

2. _____

3. _____

4. _____

5. _____

6. _____

7. _____

8. _____

9. _____

10. _____

Capitalizing Geographic Names 47

Arts & Crafts

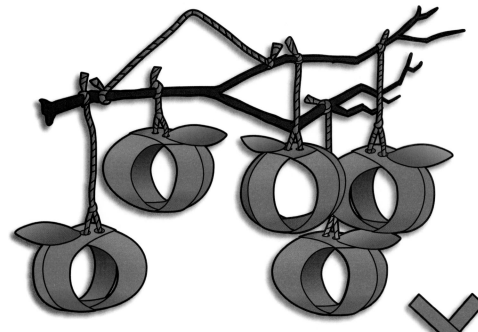

Apple Mobile

To construct this attractive fall hanging, cut a 9" x 12" sheet of red construction paper into 12 one-inch strips. Make one apple by gluing two of the strips together to form an X. Next, overlap and glue the ends together as shown. Also glue a green paper leaf to the top of the apple. Repeat for a desired number of apples. Tie each apple to a stick by punching two holes at the top of the apple and threading a length of yarn through the holes, knotting it at both ends.

"Hand-made" Sunflower

A child traces his hand on yellow construction paper five times and then cuts out the tracings. Next, he glues the cutouts to a sheet of construction paper, as shown, and adds a green paper stem and leaf. To finish off his project, the student glues sunflower seeds to the center of his flower.

Watermelon Note Holder

These sweet slices can hold scrap paper, notes, and even a pencil or two! To make a note holder, paint the back of a half paper plate green to look like a watermelon rind. Then paint the front of a whole paper plate pink and green to look like the inside of a watermelon. After the paint is dry, glue the two pieces together, as shown, and attach a few pieces of magnetic tape to the back. To use the note holder, simply fill the pocket with paper and hang it in a handy spot.

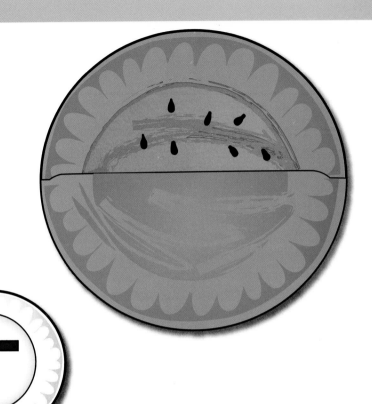

Labor Day Bank

Get students raving about saving with these personalized banks! Ask each student to bring in a cylindrical container with a lid, such as an oatmeal package. To make a bank, she cuts out magazine and flier pictures showing items she would like to have, as well as pictures showing how she could earn the money to buy the items. Then she glues the pictures on the package and uses markers to caption each one. Help her cut a slit in the lid large enough for coins and let the saving begin!

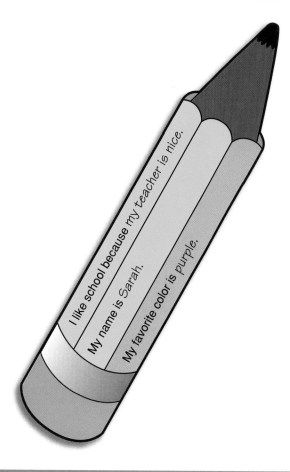

Pencil Pals

Materials for one pencil:
brown construction paper copy of the pattern below
yellow construction paper copy of page 51
¾" x 7" strip of aluminum foil
1" x 7" strip of pink construction paper
tape
glue
scissors

Steps:
1. Complete the information on the yellow pencil pattern. Then cut it out and glue where indicated.
2. Cut out and glue the brown pencil point pattern to form a cone shape.
3. Glue the pink strip and the aluminum foil strip to the base of the pencil as shown.
4. Tape the cone shape inside the top of the pencil.
5. Share the information on the pencil pal with the rest of the class.

Pencil Point Pattern
Use with "Pencil Pals" on this page.

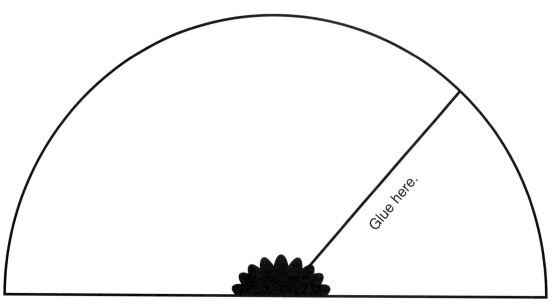

Glue here.

Use with “Pencil Pals” on page 50.

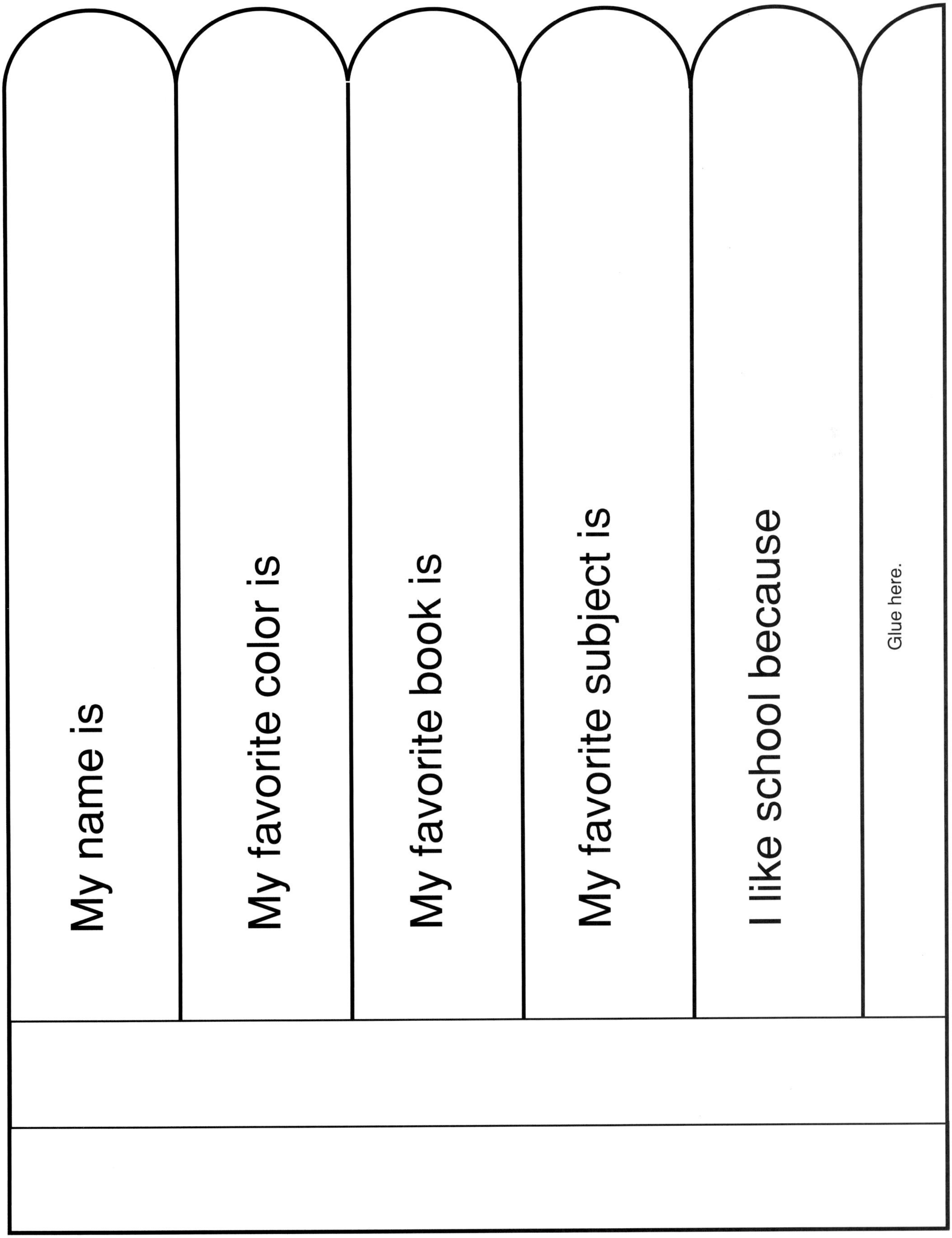
My name is
My favorite color is
My favorite book is
My favorite subject is
I like school because
Glue here.

Mount an oval-shaped racetrack on a wall. Then give each child a copy of one of the racecar patterns on page 54. (Be sure to distribute a mix of left- and right-facing cars). Have him write a sentence telling one thing he wants to learn this school year and sign his name. Also have him decorate and cut out his car. Display the cars along the track as shown.

All Revved Up to Learn!

I want to learn about space. Alan

We Work in Harmony!

Draw a music staff across a bulletin board and title it as shown. Then have each child write his name on the flag of a music note cutout (pattern on page 54) and decorate it with a colorful design. Mount the notes on trimmed black paper and arrange them in a melodious tune!

Displays

Give each child a copy of the squirrel-and-acorn-cap pattern on page 55 to personalize and cut out. Mount the patterns at the top of brown construction paper sheets as shown. Then, each week, enlist your students' help in selecting different work samples to display.

Cut a tree shape from brown butcher paper or paper grocery bags. Use a marker to add markings that resemble tree bark. Then, to give the tree a rough, textured look, crumple the cutout before mounting it on the board. Add apples, leaves, and your students' best writing!

Racecar Patterns

Use with "All Revved Up to Learn!" on page 52.

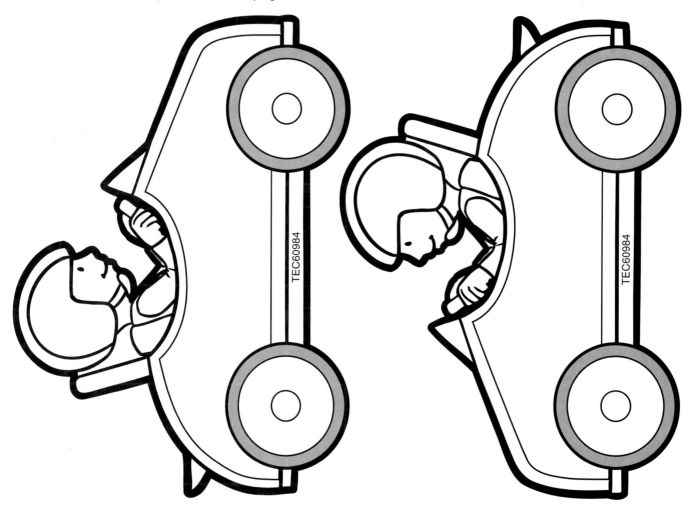

Music Note Pattern

Use with "We Work in Harmony!" on page 52.

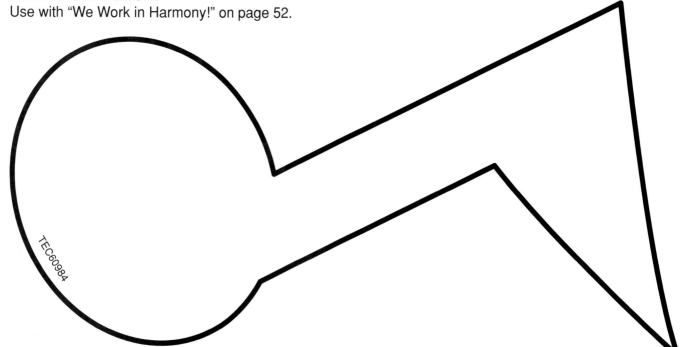

TEC60984

Centers

Basic facts

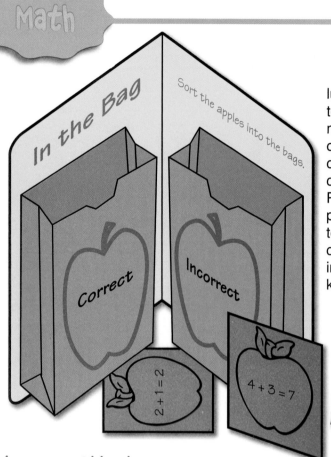

In the Bag

To make this file folder center, label two brown lunch bags "Correct" and "Incorrect." Glue the bags to the inside of a file folder labeled as shown. Then make several construction paper copies of the apple cards on page 41. Program half the apples with correct math facts (addition, subtraction, or multiplication) and the other half with incorrect math facts. Place the apples in a resealable plastic bag and paper-clip it to the folder. Also attach an answer key to the back of the folder for self-checking. To use the center, a child stands up the folder, sorts the apples into the matching bags, and then uses the answer key to check his work.

Initial consonant blends

Sunflower Power

Label two plastic flowerpots with different consonant blends, as shown. Then program the word endings on page 58 on 20 sunflower patterns (also on page 58). Tape a craft stick to the back of each flower. Place the flowers in a resealable plastic bag at a center along with the two flowerpots and a supply of paper. A student sorts the flowers into the correct flowerpots, writing each newly formed word on her paper.

Summarizing

A Story in Slices

Set up this partner center by placing copies of the watermelon slice pattern on page 58 at a center along with a few picture books, construction paper, and scissors. Each student pair selects a story and reads it aloud. Together the partners summarize the beginning, middle, and end of the story on three different watermelon slices. The twosome then cuts out and decorates a construction paper cover, labels it with the book's title, and staples it atop the stacked watermelon slices.

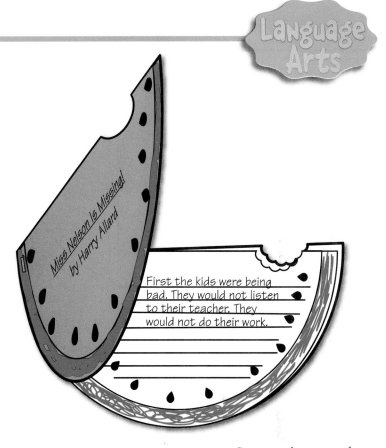

Miss Nelson Is Missing!
by Harry Allard

First the kids were being bad. They would not listen to their teacher. They would not do their work.

Math

Comparing numbers

Whooo's Greater?

Program each of 16 owl patterns from page 59 with a different two-, three-, or four-digit number. Place the owls in a paper bag at a center along with copies of the recording sheet on page 59. A child draws two owls from the bag and writes each number on an owl on her recording sheet. She writes ">" or "<" between the two numbers. Then she sets those owl cards aside and repeats the process with the remaining cards.

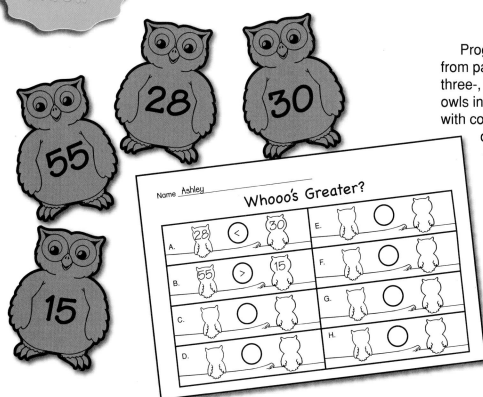

Name Ashley
Whooo's Greater?

A. 28 < 30
B. 55 > 15
C.
D.
E.
F.
G.
H.

Centers **57**

Sunflower Pattern and Word Endings

Use with "Sunflower Power" on page 56.

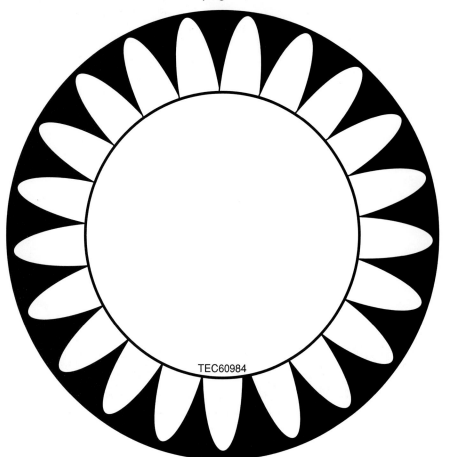

TEC60984

pl Word Endings

___ ___ane
___ ___ate
___ ___ace
___ ___at
___ ___ant
___ ___ease
___ ___um
___ ___us
___ ___enty
___ ___an

fl Word Endings

___ ___ag
___ ___ower
___ ___at
___ ___ash
___ ___oss
___ ___ake
___ ___ap
___ ___oat
___ ___ip
___ ___ame

Watermelon Pattern

Use with "A Story in Slices" on page 57.

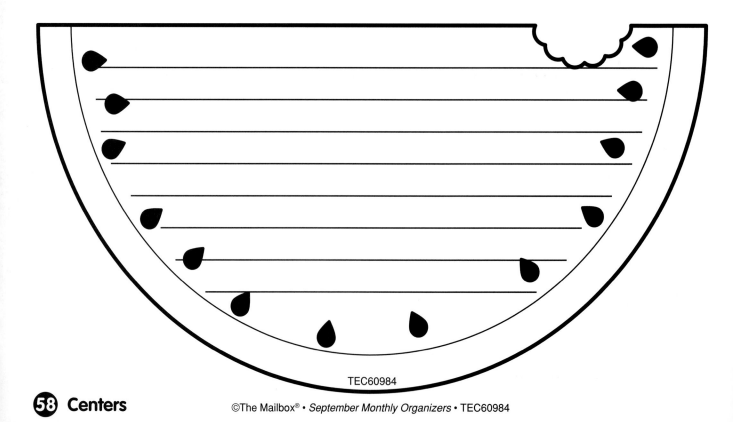

TEC60984

TEC60984   TEC60984

Name _____

Whooo's Greater?

A.

B.

C.

D.

E.

F.

G.

H.

Games

Listening

Tyrone is a swimmer.

First-Day Charades

Sharpen listening skills with this get-acquainted activity! Give each pair of students five minutes to learn each other's name and three unique things about each other, such as hobbies, unusual traits, or accomplishments. Have one set of partners at a time introduce each other to the class. Then have each partner take a turn acting out—charades style—one of the unique things he learned about his buddy. If the class does not guess correctly after three attempts, have the child reveal the answer. Then prompt the student's partner to begin her charade.

Addition and subtraction facts

Math

Tic-Tac-Toe Facts

Add a delightful twist to this popular game! Arrange nine chairs to resemble a tic-tac-toe grid. Also, program each of five large index cards with an *X* and each of five additional cards with an *O*. Divide the class into an X team and an O team. Alternating between the teams, call an addition or a subtraction fact to a player. If the player gives the correct answer, he takes a card matching his team and sits in the chair of his choice. If he gives an incorrect answer, a player from the opposing team gets to answer. Play continues until a team has three students forming tic-tac-toe in the chairs. Award that team a point and then repeat with additional rounds.

Plural nouns

A Pie Full of Plurals

Materials for each pair of students: copy of page 62, die, 2 game markers, scissors, paper, pencils

To play:
1. Players cut the answer key from the gameboard and put their markers on Start.
2. Player 1 rolls the die. If the number is odd, she moves her game marker one space. If the number is even, she moves her marker two spaces.
3. Player 1 writes the word in plural form on her paper.
4. Player 2 checks the key. If correct, Player 1 keeps her marker on that space. If incorrect, she moves her marker back one space.
5. Player 2 takes a turn.
6. The game continues in this way, alternating players, until one reaches Finish.

Math

Place value

Build It!

To prepare this small-group game, simply cut apart two copies of the cards on page 63 and place them in a resealable bag. To play, players shuffle the cards and stack them facedown in the center of the playing area. Each player draws one card from the stack; then each player draws a second card from the stack. The players place the cards number side up in front of them to create the largest number possible. The player with the largest number wins the round and earns one point. If there is a tie, each player earns a point. The first player to earn five points wins.

A Pie Full of Plurals

Start

1. apple
2. basket
3. cherry
4. pie
5. pan
6. car
7. truck
8. daisy
9. bee
10. flower
11. candy
12. lady
13. party
14. pencil
15. hand
16. tree
17. puppy
18. book
19. house
20. shirt
21. rock
22. fence
23. cloud
24. horse
25. story

Finish

©The Mailbox® • September Monthly Organizers • TEC60984

Note to the teacher: Use with "A Pie Full of Plurals" on page 61.

Games

Answer Key

1. apples
2. baskets
3. cherries
4. pies
5. pans
6. cars
7. trucks
8. daisies
9. bees
10. flowers
11. candies
12. ladies
13. parties
14. pencils
15. hands
16. trees
17. puppies
18. books
19. houses
20. shirts
21. rocks
22. fences
23. clouds
24. horses
25. stories

Management Tips

Fill the Tree!

Collect bushels of good behavior with this motivating display! Use the pattern on page 41 to make a colorful supply of apple cutouts. Every time your class receives a compliment from a staff member or demonstrates positive behavior, write the compliment on a cutout and secretly program the back with a class reward. Attach the apple to a tree on a bulletin board titled "Our Compliment Tree." When the tree has a predetermined number of apples, pick one apple off the tree and treat the class to the reward on the back.

Mascot Motivator

At the start of the school year, select a small stuffed animal to serve as your class mascot. Attach a ladder cutout to your board that leads to a laminated seasonal cutout. Each Monday morning, program the cutout with a class reward. Then use a large binder clip or clothespin to attach the mascot to the bottom rung of the ladder. Throughout the week move the mascot up rung by rung when students are modeling appropriate behavior. If the mascot reaches the top, students earn the reward!

Show samples of student work.

Include mints, small snacks, and a pitcher of water with paper cups.

Make positive remarks first and then mention the areas that need improvement.

Place chairs in a circle and keep paper and pens nearby.

Listen attentively to parents' needs.

Express appreciation for parents' time and especially for their child!

Conference Acrostic

Successful parent conferences are a few letters away! Simply keep a copy of the acrostic reminder shown on your calendar or in your lesson plan book. You'll always be prepared!

"Purr-fect"!
I'm proud of you,

_____!
student

©The Mailbox® • *September Monthly Organizers* • TEC60984

Out of This World!

_____
student

©The Mailbox® • *September Monthly Organizers* • TEC60984

★ ★ ★ ★ ★ ★ ★ ★

Gold Star Coupon
Good for

_____

_____

_____

©The Mailbox® • *September Monthly Organizers* • TEC60984

Good Apple Coupon
Good for

_____

_____

©The Mailbox® • *September Monthly Organizers* • TEC60984

You're "Z" best!

student

I'm WILD about your work!

teacher

©The Mailbox® • *September Monthly Organizers* • TEC60984

Congratulations,

_____.
student

I knew you could!
I knew you could!

teacher

date

©The Mailbox® • *September Monthly Organizers* • TEC60984

Note to the teacher: Use copies of the awards and coupons to recognize positive student work and behavior.

Time Fillers

Number Builders

Reinforce number sense with this quick challenge. Make ten copies of the apple cards on page 41 on red construction paper. Cut out the cards, label each with a different digit from 0 through 9, and then place them in a container. To play, have each child draw three boxes on her paper as shown. Explain that the goal is for her to build the largest number possible. Then take an apple from the container, announce its digit, and allow time for students to record the digit in a box. Tell students that once a digit is recorded, it cannot be moved. Repeat with two more apples. Identify the largest number and ask for a show of hands to see how many students met the challenge. If there's time for another round, have students try building the smallest number possible!

Name It!

Reinforce spelling and vowel sounds with this easy time filler. Make a list of familiar school-related words. Whenever there are spare minutes, write one listed word on the board at a time, using a blank line for one of the word's vowels. Have students raise their hands when they know the word. If needed, give a few clues to help them identify it. Then call on one child to name the item and invite another child to fill in the missing vowel.

Category Challenge

This easy-to-do listing activity sharpens fluency skills. Divide students into teams and then announce a topic similar to the ones shown. Allow teams a few minutes to list as many items as they can that fit the category. When time is up, have each group read its list. The group with the most listed items that fit the category is the winner!

Topics

Things Found in a Backpack
Things Found on the Playground
Things Seen From a School Bus
School Supplies
Activities to Do in the Fall
Areas of the School

I didn't know all that was in there!

Back-to-School ABCs

Fill a few minutes between lessons with this brainstorming activity. Have students go through the alphabet, naming words related to school. With everyone contributing, you'll go from *A* to *Z* in a flash!

apples

bus

chalk

displays

Journal Prompts

- Pretend that while you are picking apples, you find a blue apple. Write about what happens next.

- Do you think school was different for your grandparents? Explain.

- Write three things that your teacher should tell parents at open house.

- Which of these people should earn the most money: baseball player, nurse, lawyer, or carpenter? Explain.

- Fall begins in late September. Write three reasons why you will miss summer.

- Imagine that your new teacher is a cat named Ms. Meow. Describe the first day of school.

Choose one of these ready-to-go writing ideas to use with the backpack pattern on page 70.

- Guide each student to think about his strengths and talents. Give the youngster a copy of the pattern. Have him draw a picture of himself doing what he does best and then write about it.

- Program a copy of the pattern with a journal prompt from above; then make a class supply.

- Give each child a copy of the pattern and have her draw a picture of her favorite school supply in the top section. Then have her write about where, when, and how she got the item.

Daniel

I am taking karate lessons. I started taking them last year. Last year I was a white belt. Now I am a yellow belt. We get to shout when we practice our kicks.

Apple of My Eye

To set up this sentence-writing activity, share with students the idiom "You're the apple of my eye." Discuss its meaning and have each student think about a friend who is the apple of her eye. Next, give each child a red construction paper copy of the apple pattern on page 71. The student cuts out the pattern and uses it as a template to cut out three additional apples from white paper. Then she staples the red apple atop the white ones to create a booklet as shown. On each booklet page, she writes one positive action that her friend does to make herself the apple of her eye.

Ashley
is the apple
of my
eye!

My friend
listens to me.

Our Classmates in a Nutshell

This question-and-answer session reinforces ending punctuation. Copy the question-and-answer strips on page 71 so that each child has two strips. On each strip, have him write his name in the top acorn and a question that he would like to ask a classmate where indicated. Pair students. Have one partner ask his question and write his partner's name and answer on the strip; then have the duo switch roles. Repeat with different partners for the second strip. Collect the strips and post them on a bulletin board titled "We're Nuts About Our New Classmates."

Question: How many people are in your family?

Answer: There are six people in Nicole's family.

Question: Where were you born?

Answer: Kate was born in Atlanta, Georiga.

Backpack Pattern
Use with the writing ideas on page 68.

TEC60984

Writing Ideas & Prompts

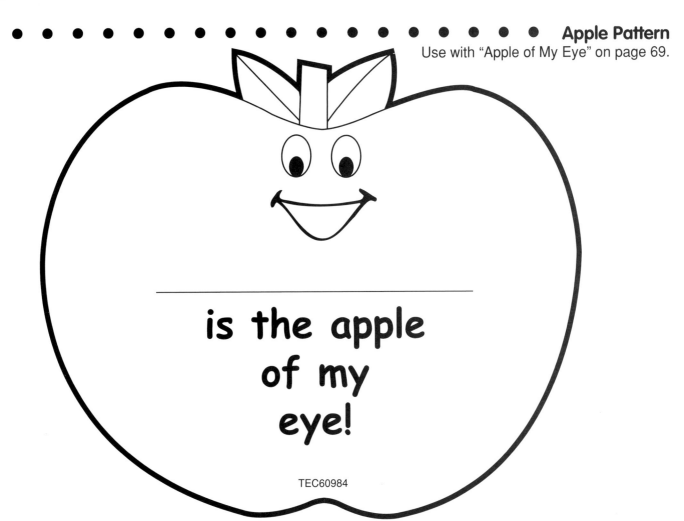

is the apple
of my
eye!

TEC60984

Question-and-Answer Strips
Use with "Our Classmates in a Nutshell" on page 69.

Question: _____

_____

Answer: _____

_____

TEC60984

Question: _____

_____

Answer: _____

_____

TEC60984

The Good Apple Show

A ready-to-use center mat and cards

Materials:

center mat to the right
center cards on page 75
copies of the recording sheet on page 77
resealable plastic bag

Preparing the centers:

Cut out the cards and store them in the plastic bag.

Using the center:

1. A student lays the cards faceup.
2. He puts three number cards that make a fact family on the mat.
3. He copies the numbers and writes the fact family on his recording sheet.
4. He removes the cards from the mat.
5. He repeats steps 2 through 4 until his recording sheet is complete.

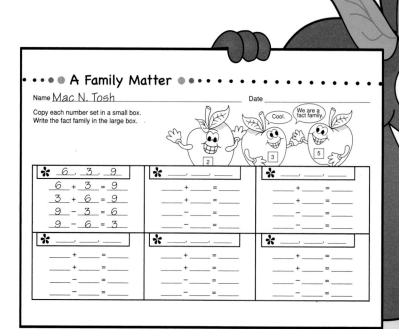

The Good Apple Show

Put three numbers that make a fact family on the mat.
Write the numbers on the recording sheet.
Remove the cards.
Repeat. Make a different fact family.

(A number from 1 to 9).

(A number from 1 to 9).

(A number from 1 to 9).

CORE TV   Channel 12

1	2	3
4	5	6
7	8	9
10	11	12
13	14	15
16	17	

The Good Apple Show
TEC60984

The Good Apple Show
TEC60984

The Good Apple Show
TEC60984

The Good Apple Show
TEC60984

The Good Apple Show
TEC60984

The Good Apple Show
TEC60984

The Good Apple Show
TEC60984

The Good Apple Show
TEC60984

The Good Apple Show
TEC60984

The Good Apple Show
TEC60984

The Good Apple Show
TEC60984

The Good Apple Show
TEC60984

The Good Apple Show
TEC60984

The Good Apple Show
TEC60984

The Good Apple Show
TEC60984

The Good Apple Show
TEC60984

A Family Matter

Name _____

Date _____

Copy each number set in a small box.
Write the fact family in the large box.

Note to the teacher: Use with the directions on page 72.

Bubba's Buses

A ready-to-use center mat and cards

Editing for beginning capitals and end marks

Materials:
center mat to the right
sentence cards on page 81
copies of the recording sheet on page 83
resealable plastic bag

Preparing the center:
Cut out the cards and store them in the plastic bag.

Using the center:
1. A student stacks the cards faceup.
2. He edits the sentence on the top card for a beginning capital letter and a correct end mark.
3. He lays the card on the appropriate box ("Correct" or "Not Correct").
4. He continues in this manner until all the cards are sorted.
5. He completes a copy of the recording sheet.

Hold on!	Bubba has a problem.
it is the first day of school.	one bus is ready to go
Look at the bus with the flat tire!	Why did that big tire go flat.
is it hard to fix a big bus tire	Bubba shakes his head.
There are animals waiting for a ride.	what will Bubba do?
Look out?	Bubba is busy.

Bubba's Buses
TEC60984

Bubba's Buses
TEC60984

Bubba's Buses
TEC60984

Bubba's Buses
TEC60984

Bubba's Buses
TEC60984

Bubba's Buses
TEC60984

Bubba's Buses
TEC60984

Bubba's Buses
TEC60984

Bubba's Buses
TEC60984

Bubba's Buses
TEC60984

Bubba's Buses
TEC60984

Bubba's Buses
TEC60984

Bubba's Buses

Name _____

Date _____

School

Gather the cards that need repairs.
A flat tire should be on the back of each one.
Write the sentences on the lines.
Make the repairs!

The bus!
The bus!

It's about time!

1. _____

2. _____

3. _____

4. _____

5. _____

6. _____

Editing for Beginning Capitals and End Marks

Note to the teacher: Use with the directions on page 78.

Colors by Number

Name_____   Date_____

Write the numbers in order from least to greatest.
The first one has been done for you.

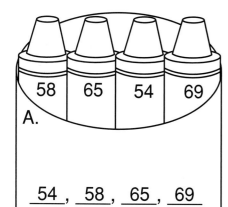

A. 58 65 54 69

_54_ , _58_ , _65_ , _69_

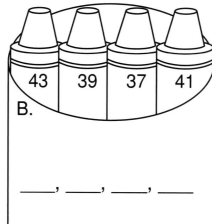

B. 43 39 37 41

____, ____, ____, ____

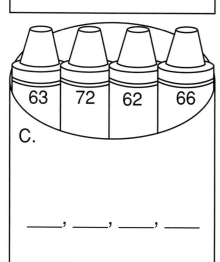

C. 63 72 62 66

____, ____, ____, ____

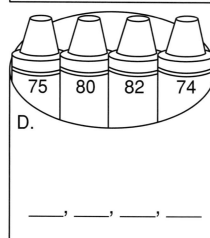

D. 75 80 82 74

____, ____, ____, ____

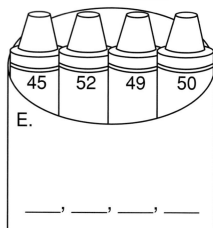

E. 45 52 49 50

____, ____, ____, ____

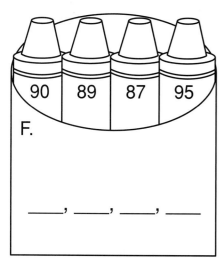

F. 90 89 87 95

____, ____, ____, ____

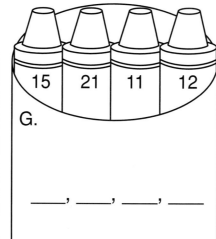

G. 15 21 11 12

____, ____, ____, ____

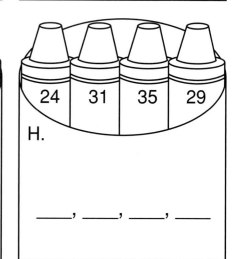

H. 24 31 35 29

____, ____, ____, ____

Sharpening Plurals

Name _____

Date _____

Add -s or -es to each singular word.
Write each plural word on the matching pencil sharpener.

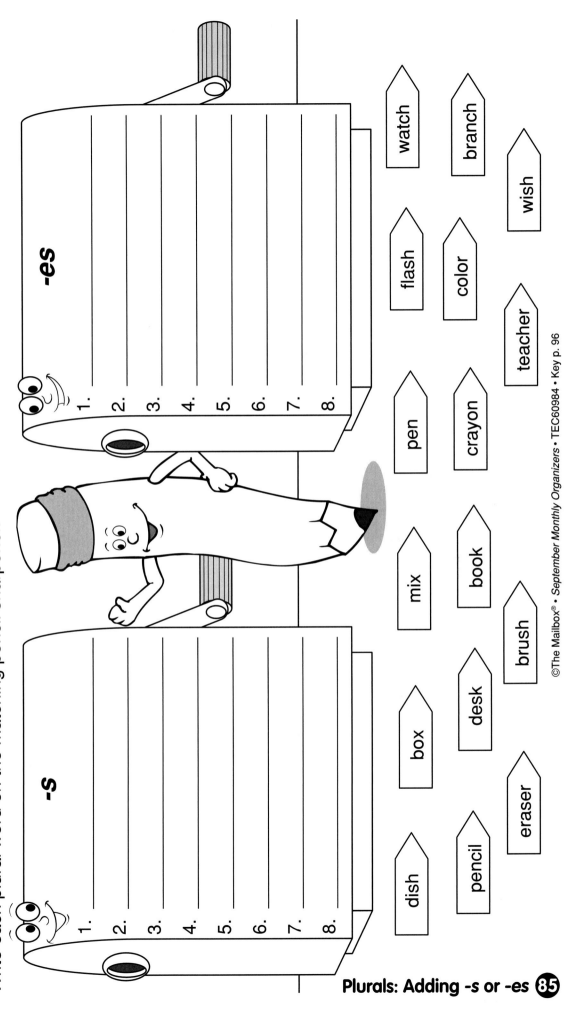

-es

1.
2.
3.
4.
5.
6.
7.
8.

-s

1.
2.
3.
4.
5.
6.
7.
8.

watch   branch   wish

flash   color   teacher

pen   crayon

mix   book   brush

box   desk

dish   pencil   eraser

©The Mailbox® • September Monthly Organizers • TEC60984 • Key p. 96

Plurals: Adding -s or -es 85

Off to Work We Go!

Name _____ Date _____

Look at the underlined word.
Color the hat by the code.

 1. Labor Day <u>honors</u> workers.

 2. <u>People</u> do many types of jobs.

 3. My father <u>writes</u> books.

 4. He is an <u>author</u>.

 5. My mother <u>works</u> in a bakery.

 6. She <u>bakes</u> pies, cakes, and cookies.

 7. My <u>teacher</u> has an important job.

 8. She <u>helps</u> children learn.

 9. I want to be a <u>doctor</u>.

 10. I want to help <u>people</u> who are sick.

11. My sister wants to be a basketball <u>player</u>.

12. She <u>loves</u> basketball!

Apple-Picking Time!

Name_____ Date_____

Circle each letter that should be capitalized.
Color an apple that shows the same letter.

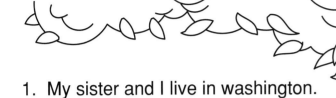

1. My sister and I live in washington.

2. We go to school at West lake.

3. our class went to pick apples.

4. I sat next to danny on the bus.

5. i wanted to pick red apples.

6. Jason and john picked green apples.

7. we had a great time.

8. I ate one of sue's apples.

9. two apples had worms in them!

10. Mr. green threw them in the trash.

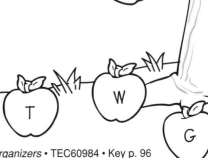

Name _____

Date _____

Nuts About Place Value

Cut apart the acorn cards below.
Glue each card on the basket that matches the value of the underlined digit.

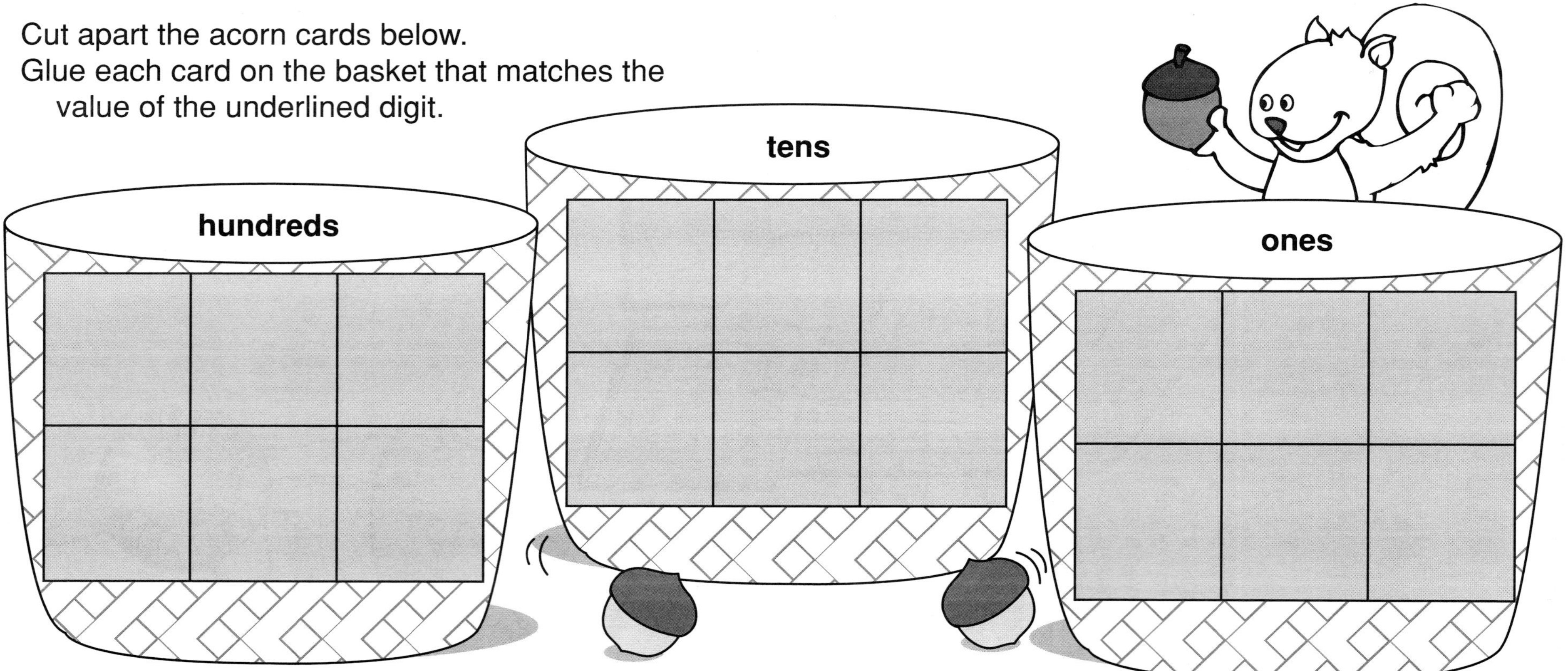

ones

tens

hundreds

©The Mailbox® • September Monthly Organizers • TEC60984 • Key p. 96

1<u>8</u>0	15<u>2</u>
67<u>8</u>	<u>8</u>09
<u>9</u>20	23<u>1</u>
5<u>3</u>8	47<u>5</u>
31<u>4</u>	7<u>9</u>2
<u>2</u>95	58<u>6</u>
3<u>8</u>6	42<u>4</u>
64<u>7</u>	<u>8</u>11
36<u>3</u>	<u>9</u>50

Place Value to 1,000

Seeds of Punctuation

Name_____ Date_____

Add the correct end mark to each sentence.
Color a matching apple.

1. Wow, look at all the trees Johnny planted

2. Johnny planted trees in Ohio and Indiana

3. Did he really give away apple seeds

4. Did Johnny wear a pot for a hat

5. Some say that Johnny didn't wear shoes

6. Do you think his feet were cold

7. His real name was John Chapman

8. Do you know that a young tree is called a sapling

9. Boy, Johnny walked a long way

10. Many people told stories about Johnny Appleseed

11. What is your favorite story

12. Have you ever told it to anyone

Up, Up, and Away

Name _____ Date _____

Subtract.

W
59
− 36
____

T
91
− 30
____

O
35
− 14
____

S
83
− 51
____

G
44
− 13
____

B
39
− 23
____

E
94
− 72
____

R
85
− 43
____

N
29
− 12
____

T
95
− 52
____

H
86
− 36
____

R
67
− 34
____

Who invented the airplane that couldn't fly?
To solve the riddle, write the letters above on the numbered lines below.

___ ___ ___   ___ ___ ___ ___ ___
43   50   22   23   42   21   17   31

___ ___ ___ ___ ___ ___ ___ ___
16   42   21   61   50   22   33   32

Two-Digit Subtraction Without Regrouping

Vocabulary

A New Word

choosesmicken

Make up a new word!

Write the word.

Write what the new word means.

Write the new word in a sentence.

Go ahead!
Make up another new word!

©The Mailbox® • September Monthly Organizers • TEC60984

Planning a story

FIDO

Whisked Away

Tell what you think is happening in the picture.

Answer each question.
1. Who?
2. What?
3. When?
4. Where?
5. Why?

If you like, use your
ideas to write a story!

©The Mailbox® • September Monthly Organizers • TEC60984

Compound words

Sunshine and Sunflower

Write ten or more different
compound words.

Write them like this:

sun + flower = sunflower

©The Mailbox® • September Monthly Organizers • TEC60984

Rhyming words

Apple Rapper

Write a rap about an apple.

Use the word bank to help you.

Word Bank
core, poor, door, floor
stem, hem, them, gem
seed, need, feed, greed
crunch, munch, bunch, lunch
red, bed, head, said

©The Mailbox® • September Monthly Organizers • TEC60984

Basic facts

Add It Up

Write ten different ways to make 10 by adding.

Use us all together!

Me too!

Use me! Use me!

©The Mailbox® • September Monthly Organizers • TEC60984

Nonstandard measurement

To the Point

Use your pencil to measure.

Measure five classroom items.

Write the name of each item and its length.

This book is one pencil long.

©The Mailbox® • September Monthly Organizers • TEC60984

Number awareness

Numbers All Around

You do many things that use numbers.

List ten different ways you used numbers in the last week.

I have 5 seeds.

There are 12 apples in my family!

©The Mailbox® • September Monthly Organizers • TEC60984

Comparing numbers

You Pick!

Write 12 number sentences.

Use each math symbol below four times.

< less than
> greater than
= equal

Like this!

242 = 242

©The Mailbox® • September Monthly Organizers • TEC60984

93

Page 27

9 + 7 = 16	6 + 7	8 + 8	8 + 4	9 + 4
6 + 6 = 12	8 + 5	6 + 8	5 + 7	1 + 5
5 + 6 = 11	3 + 6	7 + 4	9 + 4	6 + 7
6 + 8 = 14	9 + 5	3 + 6	4 + 9	5 + 5
5 + 7 = 12	6 + 6	9 + 0	8 + 3	9 + 2
3 + 4 = 7	4 + 4	2 + 5	7 + 8	6 + 6
4 + 6 = 10	5 + 3	7 + 3	3 + 8	7 + 1
7 + 7 = 14	4 + 9	2 + 5	8 + 6	2 + 8
8 + 3 = 11	7 + 6	8 + 8	5 + 9	6 + 5
1 + 5 = 6	2 + 8	4 + 7	3 + 3	9 + 2
9 + 8 = 17	5 + 5	8 + 9	7 + 3	6 + 0
3 + 6 = 9	2 + 7	7 + 7	5 + 2	4 + 4

Page 28

1. There is no school on Labor Day.
2. Ms. Stone's class visited the pumpkin patch on Tuesday.
3. Every Wednesday, Mr. Jones visits our classroom.
4. Bring a book to share each day in October!
5. Open house will be at 7:00 on Monday.
6. Mr. Lee's class will visit the firehouse on October 7.
7. The school will serve pizza each Friday in September.
8. Bring snacks for your class on September 24.
9. We will have a fall party on the last Friday in October.
10. Help us clean the playground on Saturday.

Page 29

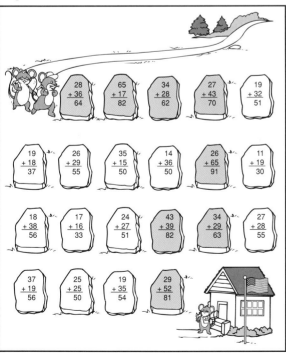

Page 42

First, peel the apples.
Then cut the apples into slices.
Next, place the apple slices in a pot of water.
Boil the slices until they are soft.
Mash the soft apples.
Finally, eat the applesauce.

Page 43

A	O	L	M	I	N
6 2 + 3 — 11	9 0 + 7 — 16	5 5 + 5 — 15	1 3 + 8 — 12	2 8 + 0 — 10	5 9 + 4 — 18

H	R	F	W	D	G
6 2 + 1 — 9	7 4 + 2 — 13	6 8 + 5 — 19	3 1 + 2 — 6	4 6 + 4 — 14	6 5 + 6 — 17

FINDING HALF A WORM!

Page 45

10 − 2 = 8	13 − 9 = 4	11 − 5 = 6
8 + 2 = 10	4 + 9 = 13	6 + 5 = 11
10 − 8 = 2	13 − 4 = 9	11 − 6 = 5
2 + 8 = 10	9 + 4 = 13	5 + 6 = 11

17 − 8 = 9	12 − 3 = 9	14 − 6 = 8
9 + 8 = 17	9 + 3 = 12	8 + 6 = 14
17 − 9 = 8	12 − 9 = 3	14 − 8 = 6
8 + 9 = 17	3 + 9 = 12	6 + 8 = 14

13 − 7 = 6	15 − 9 = 6
6 + 7 = 13	6 + 9 = 15
13 − 6 = 7	15 − 6 = 9
7 + 6 = 13	9 + 6 = 15

Page 46

1. 55	2. 38	3. 89	4. 86
5. 87	6. 49	7. 48	8. 79
9. 59	10. 78		
11. 57	12. 66		

Page 47

1. Salem, Oregon
2. Reno, Nevada
3. Flagstaff, Arizona
4. Roswell, New Mexico
5. Hays, Kansas
6. Austin, Texas
7. Jackson, Mississippi
8. Orlando, Florida
9. Richmond, Virginia
10. New York, New York

Page 83

Order may vary.
1. It is the first day of school.
2. One bus is ready to go.
3. Why did that big tire go flat?
4. Is it hard to fix a big bus tire?
5. What will Bubba do?
6. Look out!

Page 84

A. 54, 58, 65, 69
B. 37, 39, 41, 43
C. 62, 63, 66, 72
D. 74, 75, 80, 82
E. 45, 49, 50, 52
F. 87, 89, 90, 95
G. 11, 12, 15, 21
H. 24, 29, 31, 35

Page 85

Order may vary.
-s
1. desks
2. erasers
3. books
4. pencils
5. crayons
6. teachers
7. pens
8. colors

-es
1. dishes
2. boxes
3. mixes
4. watches
5. brushes
6. flashes
7. branches
8. wishes

Page 86

1. blue
2. red
3. blue
4. red
5. blue
6. blue
7. red
8. blue
9. red
10. red
11. red
12. blue

Page 87

1. My sister and I live in Washington.
2. We go to school at West Lake.
3. Our class went to pick apples.
4. I sat next to Danny on the bus.
5. I wanted to pick red apples.
6. Jason and John picked green apples.
7. We had a great time.
8. I ate one of Sue's apples.
9. Two apples had worms in them!
10. Mr. Green threw them in the trash.

Page 88

Order may vary.

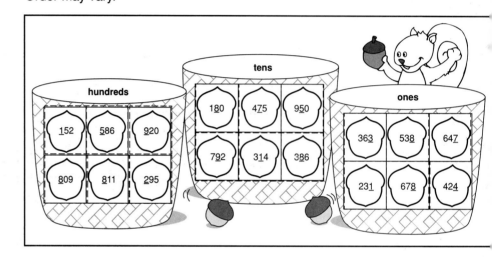

Page 89

1. !
2. .
3. ?
4. ?
5. .
6. ?
7. .
8. ?
9. !
10. .
11. ?
12. ?

Page 90

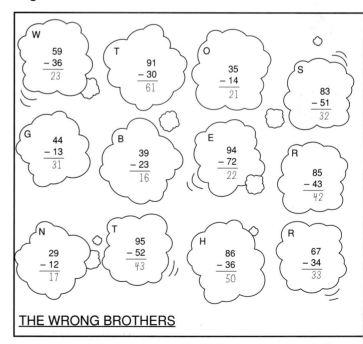

THE WRONG BROTHERS